"If we have the truth, it cannot be harmed by investigation. If we have not the truth, it ought to be harmed."

PRESIDENT J. REUBEN CLARK

To my beautiful young children…
that you may one day understand.

CES LETTER

MY SEARCH FOR ANSWERS TO
MY MORMON DOUBTS

JEREMY T. RUNNELLS

April 2013, Updated October 2017

INTRODUCTION

[Name of CES Director Removed],

Thank you for responding to my grandfather's request to answer my concerns and questions and for offering your time with me. I appreciate it.

I'm interested in your thoughts and answers as I have been unable to find official answers from the Church for most of these issues. It is my hope that you're going to have better answers than many of those given by unofficial apologists such as FairMormon and the Neal A. Maxwell Institute (formerly FARMS).

I'm just going to be straightforward in sharing my concerns. Obviously, I'm a disaffected member who lost his testimony so it's no secret which side I'm on at the moment. All this information is a result of over a year of intense research and an absolute rabid obsession with Joseph Smith and Church history. With this said, I'd be pretty arrogant and ignorant to say that I have all the information and that you don't have answers. Like you, I put my pants on one leg at a time and I see through a glass darkly. You may have new information and/or a new perspective that I may not have heard or considered before. This is why I'm genuinely interested in what your answers and thoughts are to these issues.

I've decided to put down in writing just about all the major concerns that I have. I went through my notes from my past year of research and compiled them together. It doesn't make sense for me to just lay down 5 concerns while also having 20 other concerns that legitimately challenge the truth claims of the LDS Church.

A quick description of my background might help you understand where I'm coming from. I was a very active and fully believing member my entire life up until around the summer of 2012. My grandpa already outlined my life events to you in his email so I think you get the idea that I accepted and embraced Mormonism.

In February of 2012, I was reading the news online when I came across the following news article: Mormonism Besieged by the Modern Age [1]. In the article was information about a Q&A meeting at Utah State University that LDS Church Historian and General Authority, Elder Marlin K. Jensen, gave in late 2011. He was asked his thoughts regarding the effects of Google on membership and people who are "leaving in droves" over Church history.

Elder Marlin K. Jensen's response:

> *"Maybe since Kirtland, we've never had a period of – I'll call it apostasy, like we're having now; largely over these issues…"*

This truly shocked me. I didn't understand what was going on or why people would leave "over history." I started doing research and reading books like LDS historian and scholar Richard Bushman's *Joseph Smith: Rough Stone Rolling* [2] and many others to try to better understand what was happening.

The following issues are among my main concerns.

BOOK OF MORMON
13

BOOK OF MORMON TRANSLATION
33

FIRST VISION
37

BOOK OF ABRAHAM
41

POLYGAMY | POLYANDRY
57

PROPHETS
67

KINDERHOOK PLATES & TRANSLATOR CLAIMS
77

TESTIMONY & SPIRITUAL WITNESS
81

PRIESTHOOD RESTORATION
87

WITNESSES
93

TEMPLES & FREEMASONRY
115

SCIENCE
119

OTHER CONCERNS
121

CONCLUSION
135

SOURCES | NOTES
141

EPILOGUE
143

BOOK OF MORMON
Concerns & Questions

"...the Book of Mormon is the keystone of [our] testimony. Just as the arch crumbles if the keystone is removed, so does all the Church stand or fall with the truthfulness of the Book of Mormon."

– PRESIDENT EZRA T. BENSON, *THE BOOK OF MORMON – KEYSTONE OF OUR RELIGION*[1]

"...everything in the Church – everything – rises or falls on the truthfulness of the Book of Mormon and, by implication, the Prophet Joseph Smith's account of how it came forth...It sounds like a 'sudden death' proposition to me. Either the Book of Mormon is what the Prophet Joseph said it is or this Church and its founder are false, fraudulent, a deception from the first instance onward."

– ELDER JEFFREY R. HOLLAND, "*TRUE OR FALSE*"[2], NEW ERA, JUNE 1995

1. What are 1769 King James Version edition errors[3] doing in the Book of Mormon? A purported ancient text? Errors which are unique to the 1769 edition that Joseph Smith owned?

2. When King James translators were translating the KJV Bible between 1604 and 1611, they would occasionally put in their own words into the text to make the English more readable. We know exactly what these words are because they're italicized in the KJV Bible. What are these 17th century italicized words doing in the Book of Mormon? Word for word? What does this say about the Book of Mormon being an ancient record?

ISAIAH 9:1 (KJV)

Nevertheless the dimness shall not be such as was in her vexation, when at the first he lightly afflicted the land of Zebulun and the land of Naphtali, and afterward did more grievously afflict her by the way of the sea, beyond Jordan, in Galilee of the nations.

2 NEPHI 19:1

Nevertheless, the dimness shall not be such as was in her vexation, when at first he lightly afflicted the land of Zebulun, and the land of Naphtali, and afterwards did more grievously afflict by the way of the Red Sea beyond Jordan in Galilee of the nations.

The above example, 2 Nephi 19:1[4], dated in the Book of Mormon to be around 550 BC, quotes nearly verbatim from the 1611 AD translation of Isaiah 9:1 KJV[5] – including the translators' italicized words. Additionally, the Book of Mormon describes the sea as the Red Sea. The problem with this is that (a) Christ quoted Isaiah in Matt. 4:14-15[6] and did not mention the Red Sea, (b) "Red" sea is not found in any source manuscripts, and (c) the Red Sea is 250 miles away.

MALACHI 3:10 (KJV)

...and pour you out a blessing, that there shall not be room enough to receive it.

3 NEPHI 24:10

...and pour you out a blessing that there shall not be room enough to receive it.

In the above example, the KJV translators added 7 italicized words to their English translation, which are not found in the source Hebrew manuscripts. Why does the Book of Mormon, which is supposed to have been completed by Moroni over 1,400 years prior, contain the exact identical seven italicized words of 17th century translators?

3. The Book of Mormon includes mistranslated biblical passages that were later changed in Joseph Smith's translation of the Bible. These Book of Mormon verses should match the inspired JST version instead of the incorrect KJV version that Joseph later fixed. A typical example of the differences between the BOM, the KJV, and the JST:

3 NEPHI 13:25-27 [7]

25: …Therefore I say unto you, take no thought for your life, what ye shall eat, or what ye shall drink; nor yet for your body, what ye shall put on. Is not the life more than meat, and the body than raiment?

26: Behold the fowls of the air, for they sow not, neither do they reap nor gather into barns; yet your heavenly Father feedeth them. Are ye not much better than they?

27: Which of you by taking thought can add one cubit unto his stature?

MATTHEW 6:25-27 [8]

(From the King James Version Bible – not the JST)

25: Therefore I say unto you, Take no thought for your life, what ye shall eat, or what ye shall drink; nor yet for your body, what ye shall put on. Is not the life more than meat, and the body than raiment?

26: Behold the fowls of the air: for they sow not, neither do they reap, nor gather into barns; yet your heavenly Father feedeth them. Are ye not much better than they?

27: Which of you by taking thought can add one cubit unto his stature?

MATTHEW 6:25-27 [9]

(Joseph Smith Translation of the same passages in the LDS Bible)

25: And, again, I say unto you, Go ye into the world, and care not for the world: for the world will hate you, and will persecute you, and will turn you out of their synagogues.

26: Nevertheless, ye shall go forth from house to house, teaching the people; and I will go before you.

27: And your heavenly Father will provide for you, whatsoever things ye need for food, what ye shall eat; and for raiment, what ye shall wear or put on.

Christ's Sermon on the Mount in the Bible and the Book of Mormon are identical. But Joseph Smith later corrected the Bible. In doing so, he also contradicted the same identical Sermon on the Mount passage in the Book of Mormon. The Book of Mormon is "the most correct book" and was translated a mere decade before the JST. The Book of Mormon was not corrupted over time and did not need correcting. How is it that the Book of Mormon has the incorrect Sermon on the Mount passage and does not match the correct JST version in the first place?

4. DNA analysis[10] has concluded that Native American Indians do not originate from the Middle East or from Israelites but rather from Asia. Why did the Church change the following section of the introduction page in the 2006 edition[11] Book of Mormon, shortly after the DNA results were released?

> "...the Lamanites, and they are *the principal* ancestors of the American Indians"
> to
> "...the Lamanites, and they are *among the* ancestors of the American Indians"

UPDATE: The Church conceded in its January 2014 *Book of Mormon and DNA Studies*[12] essay that the majority of Native Americans carry largely Asian DNA. The Church, through this essay, makes a major shift in narrative from its past dominant narrative and claims of the origins of the Native American Indians.

5. Anachronisms: Horses, cattle, oxen, sheep, swine, goats, elephants, wheels, chariots, wheat, silk, steel, and iron did not exist in pre-Columbian America[13] during Book of Mormon times. Why are these things mentioned in the Book of Mormon as being made available in the Americas between 2200 BC - 421 AD?

Unofficial apologists claim victories in some of these items but closer inspection reveals significant problems. It has been documented that apologists have manipulated wording so that steel is not steel, sheep become never-domesticated bighorn sheep, horses become tapirs, etc.

6. Archaeology: There is absolutely no archaeological evidence[14] to directly support the Book of Mormon or the Nephites and Lamanites, who were supposed to have numbered in the millions. This is one of the reasons why unofficial apologists have developed the Limited Geography Model[15] (it happened in Central or South America) and claim that the Hill Cumorah mentioned as the final battle of the Nephites is not in Palmyra, New York but is elsewhere. This is in direct contradiction to what Joseph Smith and other prophets have taught[16]. It also makes little sense in light of the Church's visitor's center near the Hill Cumorah in New York and the annual Church-sponsored Hill Cumorah pageants.

We read about two major war battles that took place at the Hill Cumorah (Ramah to the Jaredites) with deaths numbering in the tens of thousands – the last battle between Lamanites and Nephites around 400 AD claimed at least 230,000 deaths on the Nephite side alone. No bones, hair, chariots, swords, armor, or any other evidence of a battle whatsoever has been found at this site. John E. Clark, director of BYU's archaeological organization, wrote in the *Journal of Book of Mormon Studies*[17]:

> "In accord with these general observations about New York and Pennsylvania, we come to our principal object – the Hill Cumorah. Archaeologically speaking, it is a clean hill. No artifacts, no walls, no trenches, no arrowheads. The area immediately surrounding the hill is similarly clean. Pre-Columbian people did not settle or build here. This is not the place of Mormon's last stand. We must look elsewhere for that hill."

Compare this with the archaeological evidence of other hillside battle sites. Caerau Hillfort[18], in the Wales capital of Cardiff, was found to have abundant archaeological evidence of inhabitants and weapons of war dating as far back as 3600 BC in the form of stone arrowheads, tools, and pottery.

Compare the absent evidence of Book of Mormon civilizations to the archaeological remains of other past civilizations such as the Roman occupation of Britain[19] and other countries. There are abundant evidences of their presence during the first 400 years AD such as villas, mosaic floors, public baths, armor, weapons, writings, art, pottery, and so on. Even the major road systems used today in some of these occupied countries were built by the Romans. Additionally, there is ample evidence of the Mayan and Aztec civilizations as well as a civilization in current day Texas that dates back at least 15,000 years[20]. Another recent discovery has been made of a 14,000-year-old village in Canada[20a].

Admittedly, absence of evidence is not evidence of absence, but where are the Nephite or Lamanite buildings, roads, armors, swords, pottery, art, etc.? How can these great civilizations just vanish without a trace? Latter-day Saint Thomas Stuart Ferguson was the founder of BYU's archaeology division (New World Archaeological Foundation). NWAF was financed by the LDS Church. NWAF and Ferguson were tasked by BYU and the Church in the 1950s and 1960s to find archaeological evidence[21] to support the Book of Mormon. After 17 years of diligent effort, this is what Ferguson wrote in a February 20, 1976[22] letter about trying to dig up evidence for the Book of Mormon:

> "...you can't set Book of Mormon geography down anywhere – because it is fictional and will never meet the requirements of the dirt-archaeology.

I should say – what is in the ground will never conform to what is in the book."

7. Book of Mormon Geography: Many Book of Mormon names and places are strikingly similar to many local names and places of the region where Joseph Smith lived.

The following two maps show Book of Mormon geography compared to Joseph Smith's geography.

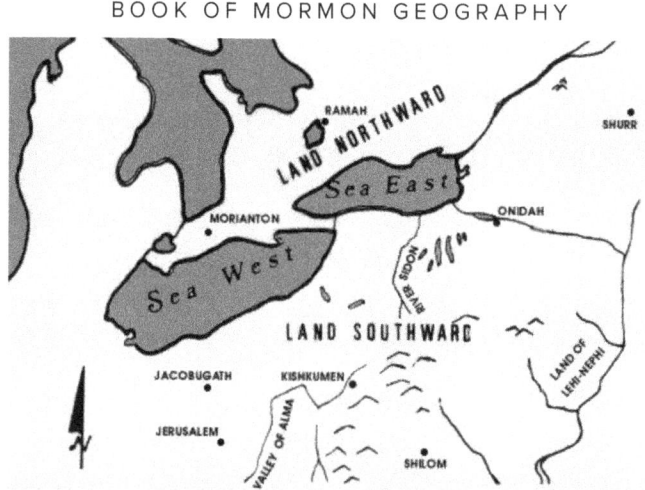

BOOK OF MORMON GEOGRAPHY

JOSEPH SMITH'S GEOGRAPHY
(Northeast United States & Southeast Canada)

The first map is the "proposed map," constructed from internal comparisons in the Book of Mormon.

18   *Book of Mormon*

Throughout the Book of Mormon we read of such features as "The Narrow Neck of Land" which was a day and a half's journey (roughly 30 miles) separating two great seas. We also read about the Hill Onidah and the Hill Ramah – all place names in the land of Joseph Smith's youth.

We read in the Book of Mormon of the city of Teancum named for a warrior named Teancum who helped General Moroni fight in the Land of Desolation. In Joseph's era, an Indian Chief named Tecumseh[23] fought and died near the narrow neck of land in helping the British in the War of 1812. Today, the city Tecumseh[24] (near the narrow neck of land) is named after this Chief.

We see the Book of Mormon city Kishkumen located near an area named, on modern maps, as Kiskiminetas[25]. There are more than a dozen Book of Mormon names that are the same as or nearly the same as modern geographical locations.

MODERN GEOGRAPHIC PLACE	BOOK OF MORMON NAME
Alma	Alma, Valley of
Antrim	Antum
Antioch	Ani-Anti
Boaz	Boaz
Hellam	Helam
Jacobsburg	Jacobugath
Jerusalem	Jerusalem
Jordan	Jordan
Kishkiminetas	Kishkumen
Lehigh	Lehi
Mantua	Manti
Moraviantown	Morianton
Noah Lakes	Noah, Land of
Oneida	Onidah
Oneida Castle	Onidah, Hill
Rama	Ramah
Ripple Lake	Ripliancum, Waters of
Sodom	Sidom
Shiloh	Shilom
Sherbrooke	Shurr

Source: Book of Mormon Authorship: A Closer Look, Vernal Holley

Why are there so many names similar to Book of Mormon names in the region where Joseph Smith lived? Is this really all just a coincidence?

UPDATE: Additional information and analysis can be found at cesletter.org/maps

HILL CUMORAH

Off the eastern coast of Mozambique in Africa is an island country called "Comoros[26]." Prior to its French occupation in 1841, the islands were known by its Arabic name, "Camora." There is an 1808 map of Africa that refers to the islands as "Camora."

Camora is near center in the above 1808 Map of Africa[27]

The largest city and capital of Comoros (formerly "Camora")? Moroni[28]. "Camora" and settlement "Moroni" were names in pirate and treasure hunting stories involving Captain William Kidd (a pirate and treasure hunter) which many 19th century New Englanders – especially treasure hunters – were familiar with.

In fact, the uniform spelling for Hill Cumorah in the 1830 edition of the Book of Mormon is spelled "Camorah[29]."

Pomeroy Tucker was born in Palmyra, New York in 1802, three years before Joseph Smith. He is considered to be a contemporary source. This is what he said about Joseph Smith:

> "Joseph ... had learned to read comprehensively ... [reading] works of fiction and records of criminality, such for instance as would be classed with the 'dime novels' of the present day. The stories of Stephen Buroughs and Captain Kidd, and the like, presented the highest charms for his expanding mental perceptions."
> – *Mormonism: Its Origin, Rise, and Progress*, p.17 [30]

Some apologists say that Tucker's *Mormonism: Its Origin, Rise, and Progress* is "anti-Mormon" and thus anything in the book cannot be trusted. If this is true, why then did LDS scholar and Church History compiler B.H. Roberts quote Tucker for background information on Joseph Smith? Also, FairMormon has an article [31] in which they quote Tucker's book 4 times as support for Joseph, and they even refer to Tucker as an "eyewitness" to Joseph and his family. Is Tucker's peripheral information only useful and accurate when it shows Joseph and the Church in a positive and favorable light?

> "We are sorry to observe, even in this enlightened age, so prevalent a disposition to credit the accounts of the marvellous. Even the frightful stories of money being hid under the surface of the earth, and enchanted by the Devil or Robert Kidd [Captain Kidd], are received by many of our respectable fellow citizens as truths."
> – *Wayne Sentinel*, Palmyra, New York, February 16, 1825 [32]

Notice that this is considered "prevalent" and "received by many of our respectable fellow citizens as truths." The above contemporary newspaper quote from Palmyra, New York, in 1825 was not tainted by any desire to damage Joseph Smith. This article provides a snapshot of the worldview of 1825 New England.

The Hill Cumorah and Moroni have absolutely nothing to do with Camora and Moroni from Captain Kidd stories? Stories that Joseph and his treasure hunting family, friends, and community were familiar with? The original 1830 Book of Mormon just happens to have the uniform "Camorah" spelling? This is all just a mere coincidence?

UPDATE: Additional information and analysis can be found at cesletter.org/cumorah

8. There was a book published in 1823 Vermont entitled *View of the Hebrews* [33]. Below is a chart

comparing the *View of the Hebrews* to the Book of Mormon:

	VIEW OF THE HEBREWS Online Source [34]	BOOK OF MORMON Online Source [35]
Published	1823, first edition 1825, second edition	1830, first edition
Location	Vermont Poultney, Rutland County **NOTE:** Oliver Cowdery, one of the Book of Mormon witnesses, lived in Poultney when **View of the Hebrews** was published.	Vermont Sharon, Windsor County **NOTE:** Windsor County is adjacent to Rutland County.
The destruction of Jerusalem	✓	✓
The scattering of Israel	✓	✓
The restoration of the Ten Tribes	✓	✓
Hebrews leave the Old World for the New World	✓	✓
Religion a motivating factor	✓	✓
Migrations a long journey	✓	✓
Encounter "seas" of "many waters"	✓	✓
The Americas an uninhabited land	✓	✓
Settlers journey northward	✓	✓
Encounter a valley of a great river	✓	✓

A unity of race (Hebrew) settle the land and are the ancestral origin of American Indians	✓	✓
Hebrew the origin of Indian language	✓	✓
Egyptian hieroglyphics	✓	✓
Lost Indian records	✓	✓
	A set of "yellow leaves" buried in Indian hill. Elder B.H. Roberts noted the "leaves" may be gold.	Joseph Smith claimed the gold plates were buried in Hill Cumorah.
Breastplate, Urim & Thummim	✓	✓
Prophets, spiritually gifted men transmit generational records	✓	✓
A man standing on a wall warning the people saying, "Wo, wo to this city…to this people" while subsequently being attacked.	✓ Jesus, son of Ananus, stood on the wall saying "Wo, wo to this city, this temple, and this people." - Came to preach for many days - Went upon a wall - Cried with a loud voice - Preached of destruction of Jerusalem - Had stones cast at him (View of Hebrews, p.20)[36]	✓ Samuel the Lamanite stood on the wall saying "Wo, wo to this city" or "this people". - Came to preach for many days - Went upon a wall - Cried with a loud voice - Preached of destruction of Nephites - Had stones cast at him (Helaman 13-16)[37]

The Gospel preached in the Americas	✓	✓
Quotes whole chapters of Isaiah	✓	✓
Good and bad are a necessary opposition	✓	✓
Pride denounced	✓	✓
Polygamy denounced	✓	✓
Sacred towers and high places	✓	✓
Messiah visits the Americas	✓	✓
	Quetzalcoatl, the white bearded "Mexican Messiah"	
Idolatry and human sacrifice	✓	✓
Hebrews divide into two classes, civilized and barbarous	✓	✓
Civilized thrive in art, written language, metallurgy, navigation	✓	✓
Government changes from monarchy to republic	✓	✓
Civil and ecclesiastical power is united in the same person	✓	✓
Long wars break out between the civilized and barbarous	✓	✓
Extensive military fortifications, observations, "watch towers"	✓	✓

Barbarous exterminate the civilized	✓	✓
Discusses the United States	✓	✓
Ethan/Ether	✓	✓
	Elder B.H. Roberts noted: "Ethan is prominently connected with the recording of the matter in the one case, and Ether in the other."	

Source: B.H. Roberts, *Studies of the Book of Mormon*, p.240-242,324-344

Reverend Ethan Smith was the author of *View of the Hebrews*. Ethan Smith was a pastor in Poultney, Vermont when he wrote and published the book. Oliver Cowdery – also a Poultney, Vermont resident – was a member of Ethan's congregation[38] during this time and before he went to New York to join his distant cousin[39] Joseph Smith. As you know, Oliver Cowdery played an instrumental role in the production of the Book of Mormon.

This direct link between Joseph and Oliver and *View of the Hebrews* demonstrates that Joseph is very likely to have been aware of the theme and content of that book. It gives weight to all the similarities described in the preceding comparison chart. Apologists may point out that the Book of Mormon is not a direct, word-for-word plagiarism of *View of the Hebrews*, and indeed that is not the claim. Rather, the similarities should give any reader pause that two books so similar in theme and content would coincidentally be connected by Oliver Cowdery.

LDS General Authority and scholar Elder B.H. Roberts[40] privately researched the link between the Book of Mormon and the *View of the Hebrews*, Joseph's father having the same dream in 1811 as Lehi's dream[41], and other sources that were available to Joseph Smith, Oliver Cowdery, Martin Harris and others before the publication of the Book of Mormon. Elder Roberts' private research was meant only for the eyes of the First

Presidency and the Quorum of the Twelve and was never intended to be available to the public. However, Roberts' work was later published [42] in 1985 as *Studies of the Book of Mormon* [43]. Based upon his research, Elder B.H. Roberts came to the following conclusion on the *View of the Hebrews*:

> "Did Ethan Smith's View of the Hebrews furnish structural material for Joseph Smith's Book of Mormon? It has been pointed out in these pages that there are many things in the former book that might well have suggested many major things in the other. Not a few things merely, one or two, or a half dozen, but many; and it is this fact of many things of similarity and the cumulative force of them that makes them so serious a menace to Joseph Smith's story of the Book of Mormon's origin."
> – B.H. Roberts, *Studies of the Book of Mormon*, p.240

While this does not prove that the Book of Mormon was plagiarized from the *View of the Hebrews*, it does demonstrate that key elements of the story of the Book of Mormon – i.e. Native Americans as Hebrew descendants, ancient records of natives preserved, scattering and gathering of Israel, Hebrew origin of Native American language, etc. pre-dated the Book of Mormon and were already among the ideas circulating among New England protestant Americans.

With these ideas already existing and the previously cited issues with KJV plagiarism, errors, anachronisms, geography problems, and more issues to come, is it unreasonable to question Joseph Smith's story of the Book of Mormon origins as Church Historian B.H. Roberts did?

UPDATE: Additional information and analysis can be found at cesletter.org/voh

9. *The Late War Between the United States and Great Britain* [44]: This book was an 1819 textbook written for New York state school children. The book depicted the events of the War of 1812 and it was specifically written in a Jacobean English style to imitate the King James Bible. This affected scriptural style was calculated to elevate the moral themes, characters and events depicted in the narrative to inspire the readers to "patriotism and piety." Readers already accustomed to revere scriptural sounding texts in the ancient Bible would be predisposed to revere this history book which employs the same linguistic style.

The first chapter [45] alone is stunning as it reads incredibly like the Book of Mormon:

1: Now it came to pass, in the one thousand eight hundred and twelfth year of the christian era, and in the thirty and sixth year after the people of the provinces of Columbia had declared themselves a free and independent nation;

2: That in the sixth month of the same year, on the first day of the month, the chief Governor, whom the people had chosen to rule over the land of Columbia;

3: Even James, whose sir-name was Madison, delivered a written paper to the Great Sannhedrim of the people, who were assembled together.

4: And the name of the city where the people were gathered together was called after the name of the chief captain of the land of Columbia, whose fame extendeth to the uttermost parts of the earth; albeit, he had slept with his fathers…

In addition to the above KJV language style present throughout the book, what are the following Book of Mormon verbatim phrases, themes, and storylines doing in a children's school textbook that was used in Joseph Smith's own time and backyard – all of this a mere decade before the publication of the Book of Mormon?

- Devices of "curious workmanship" in relation to boats and weapons.
- A "stripling" soldier "with his "weapon of war in his hand."
- "A certain chief captain…was given in trust a band of more than two thousand chosen men, to go forth to battle" and who "all gave their services freely for the good of their country."
- Fortifications: "the people began to fortify themselves and entrench the high Places round about the city."
- Objects made "partly of brass and partly of iron, and were cunningly contrived with curious works, like unto a clock; and as it were a large ball."
- "Their polished steels of fine workmanship."
- "Nevertheless, it was so that the freeman came to the defence of the city, built strong holds and forts and raised up fortifications in abundance."
- Three Indian Prophets.
- "Rod of iron."
- War between the wicked and righteous.
- Maintaining the standard of liberty with righteousness.

- Righteous Indians vs. savage Indians.
- False Indian prophets.
- Conversion of Indians.
- Bands of robbers/pirates marauding the righteous protagonists.
- Engraving records.
- "And it came to pass, that a great multitude flocked to the banners of the great Sanhedrim" compared to Alma 62:5: "And it came to pass that thousands did flock unto his standard, and did take up their swords in defense of their freedom…"
- Worthiness of Christopher Columbus.
- Ships crossing the ocean.
- A battle at a fort where righteous white protagonists are attacked by an army made up of dark-skinned natives driven by a white military leader. White protagonists are prepared for battle and slaughter their opponents to such an extent that they fill the trenches surrounding the fort with dead bodies. The surviving elements flee into the wilderness/forest.
- Cataclysmic earthquake followed by great darkness.
- Elephants/mammoths in America.
- Literary Hebraisms/Chiasmus.
- Boats and barges built from trees after the fashion of the ark.
- A bunch of "it came to pass."
- Many, many more parallels [46].

The parallels and similarities to the Book of Mormon are astounding. This web page [47] outlines very clearly and simply just how phenomenally unlikely it is that so many common rare phrases and themes could be found between these books without the *Late War* having had some influence on the Book of Mormon.

Former BYU Library Bibliographic Dept. Chairman and antique book specialist Rick Grunder states in his analysis of *The Late War* (p.770) [48]:

> "The presence of Hebraisms and other striking parallels in a popular children's textbook (Late War), on the other hand – so close to Joseph Smith in his youth – must sober our perspective."

10. Another fascinating book published in 1809, *The First Book of Napoleon* [49]:

The first chapter [50]:

> 1. And behold it came to pass, in these latter days, that an evil spirit arose on the face of the earth, and greatly troubled the sons of men.
>
> 2. And this spirit seized upon, and spread amongst the people who dwell in the land of Gaul.
>
> 3. Now, in this people the fear of the Lord had not been for many generations, and they had become a corrupt and perverse people; and their chief priests, and the nobles of the land, and the learned men thereof, had become wicked in the imagines of their hearts, and in the practices of their lives.
>
> 4. And the evil spirit went abroad amongst the people, and they raged like unto the heathen, and they rose up against their lawful king, and slew him, and his queen also, and the prince their son; yea, verily, with a cruel and bloody death.
>
> 5. And they moreover smote, with mighty wrath, the king's guards, and banished the priests, and nobles of the land, and seized upon, and took unto themselves, their inheritances, their gold and silver, corn and oil, and whatsoever belonged unto them.
>
> 6. Now it came to pass, that the nation of the Gauls continued to be sorely troubled and vexed, and the evil spirit whispered unto the people, even unto the meanest and vilest thereof...

...and it continues on. It's like reading from the Book of Mormon. When I first read this along with other passages from *The First Book of Napoleon*, I was floored. Here we have two early 19th century contemporary books written at least a decade before the Book of Mormon that not only read and sound like the Book of Mormon but also contain so many of the Book of Mormon's parallels and themes as well.

The following is a side-by-side comparison of selected phrases the Book of Mormon is known for from the beginning portion of the Book of Mormon with the same order in the beginning portion of *The First Book of Napoleon* (note: these are not direct paragraphs):

THE FIRST BOOK OF NAPOLEON

Condemn not the (writing)...an account...the First Book of Napoleon... upon the face of the earth...it came to pass...the land...their inheritances their gold and silver and…the commandments of the Lord…the foolish imaginations of their hearts…small in stature…Jerusalem…because of the perverse wickedness of the people.

BOOK OF MORMON

Condemn not the (writing)…an account…the First Book of Nephi… upon the face of the earth…it came to pass…the land…his inheritance and his gold and his silver and…the commandments of the Lord…the foolish imaginations of his heart…large in stature…Jerusalem…because of the wickedness of the people.

11. The Book of Mormon taught and still teaches a Trinitarian view of the Godhead. Joseph Smith's early theology also held this view. As part of the over 100,000 changes [51] to the Book of Mormon, there were major changes made to reflect Joseph's evolved view of the Godhead.

ORIGINAL 1830 EDITION TEXT View Online [52]	CURRENT, ALTERED TEXT View Online [53]
1 Nephi 3 (p.25) [54] And he said unto me, Behold, the virgin whom thou seest, is **the mother of God**, after the manner of the flesh.	1 Nephi 11:18 [55] And he said unto me: Behold, the virgin whom thou seest is **the mother of** the Son of **God**, after the manner of the flesh.
1 Nephi 3 (p.25) [56] And the angel said unto me, behold the Lamb of God, yea, even **the Eternal Father!**	1 Nephi 11:21 [57] And the angel said unto me: Behold the Lamb of God, yea, even the Son of **the Eternal Father**
1 Nephi 3 (p.26) [58] And I looked and beheld the Lamb of God, that he was taken by the people; yea, **the Everlasting God**, was judged of the world;	1 Nephi 11:32 [59] And I looked and beheld the Lamb of God, that he was taken by the people; yea, the Son of **the everlasting God** was judged of the world;

1 Nephi 3 (p.32) [60]	1 Nephi 13:40 [61]
*These last records…shall make known to all kindreds, tongues, and people, that the Lamb of God is **the Eternal Father and the Savior of the world**;*	*These last records…shall make known to all kindreds, tongues, and people, that the Lamb of God is **the Son of** **the Eternal Father, and the Savior of the world**;*

In addition to these revised passages, the following verses are among many verses still in the Book of Mormon that can be read with a Trinitarian view of the Godhead:

ALMA 11:38-39 [62]

38: *Now Zeezrom saith again unto him: Is the Son of God the very Eternal Father?*

39: *And Amulek said unto him: Yea, he is the very Eternal Father of heaven and of earth, and all things which in them are; he is the beginning and the end, the first and the last;*

MOSIAH 15:1-4 [63]

1: *And now Abinadi said unto them: I would that ye should understand that God himself shall come down among the children of men, and shall redeem his people.*

2: *And because he dwelleth in flesh he shall be called the Son of God, and having subjected the flesh to the will of the Father, being the Father and the Son –*

3: *The Father, because he was conceived by the power of God; and the Son, because of the flesh; thus becoming the Father and Son –*

4: *And they are one God, yea, the very Eternal Father of heaven and of earth.*

ETHER 3:14-15 [64]

14: *Behold, I am he who was prepared from the foundation of the world to redeem my people. Behold, I am Jesus Christ. I am the Father and the Son. In me shall all mankind have life, and that eternally, even they who shall believe on my name; and they shall become my sons and my daughters.*

15: *And never have I showed myself unto man whom I have created, for never has man believed in me as thou hast. Seest thou that ye are created after mine own image? Yea, even all men were created in the beginning after mine own image.*

MOSIAH 16:15 [65]

15: *"Teach them that redemption cometh through Christ the Lord, who is the very Eternal Father. Amen."*

Boyd Kirkland made the following observation [66]:

"The Book of Mormon and early revelations of Joseph Smith do indeed vividly portray a picture of the Father and Son as the same God…why is it that the Book of Mormon not only doesn't clear up questions about the Godhead which have raged in Christianity for centuries, but on the contrary just adds to the confusion? This seems particularly ironic, since a major avowed purpose of the book was to restore lost truths and end doctrinal controversies caused by the "great and abominable Church's" corruption of the Bible…In later years he [Joseph] reversed his earlier efforts to completely 'monotheise' the godhead and instead 'tritheised' it."

UPDATE: Additional information and analysis can be found at cesletter.org/trinitarian

Assuming that the official 1838 first vision account [67] is truthful and accurate, why would Joseph Smith hold a Trinitarian view of the Godhead if he personally saw God the Father and Jesus Christ as separate and embodied beings a few years earlier in the Sacred Grove?

BOOK OF MORMON TRANSLATION
Concerns & Questions

"I will begin by saying that we still have pictures on our Ward bulletin boards of Joseph Smith with the Gold Plates in front of him. That has become an irksome point and I think it is something the church should pay attention to. Because anyone who studies the history knows that is not what happened. There is no church historian who says that is what happened and yet it is being propagated by the church and it feeds into the notion that the church is trying to cover up embarrassing episodes and is sort of prettifying its own history.

So, I think we ought to just stop that immediately. I am not sure we need a lot of pictures in our chapels of Joseph looking into his hat, but we certainly should tell our children that is how it worked... It's weird. It's a weird picture. It implies it's like darkening a room when we show slides. It implies that there is an image appearing in that stone and the light would make it more difficult to see that image. So, that implies a translation that's a reading and so gives us a little clue about the whole translation process. It also raises the strange question, **'What in the world are the plates for? Why do we need them on the table if they are just wrapped up into a cloth while he looks into a seer stone?'"**

— RICHARD BUSHMAN, LDS SCHOLAR, HISTORIAN, PATRIARCH
FAIRMORMON PODCAST, EPISODE 3: RICHARD L. BUSHMAN P.1, 47:25 [1]

Unlike the story I've been taught in Sunday School, Priesthood, General Conferences, Seminary, EFY, *Ensigns*, Church history tour, Missionary Training Center, and BYU... Joseph Smith used a rock in a hat for translating[2] the Book of Mormon.

In other words, Joseph used the same magic device or "Ouija Board" that he used during his treasure hunting[3] days. He put a rock – called a "peep stone" – in his hat and put his face in the hat to tell his customers the location of buried treasure on their property. He also used this same method for translating the Book of Mormon, while the gold plates were covered, placed in another room, or even buried in the woods. The gold plates were not used for the Book of Mormon we have today.

UPDATE: These facts are now officially confirmed in the Church's December 2013 *Book of Mormon Translation*[4] essay. The Church later admitted these facts in its October 2015 *Ensign*[5], where they include a photograph of the actual rock that Joseph Smith used to place in his hat for the Book of Mormon translation. Additional photos of the rock can be viewed on lds.org[6]. In June 2016, President Dieter F. Uchtdorf posted on his Facebook page comparing the seer stone in the hat Book of Mormon translation to his iPhone[7]. FairMormon posted new Book of Mormon translation artwork[8] showing Joseph Smith's face in a hat.

BOOK OF MORMON TRANSLATION THAT THE CHURCH PORTRAYED AND STILL PORTRAYS TO ITS MEMBERS:

34   *Book of Mormon Translation*

BOOK OF MORMON TRANSLATION
AS IT ACTUALLY HAPPENED

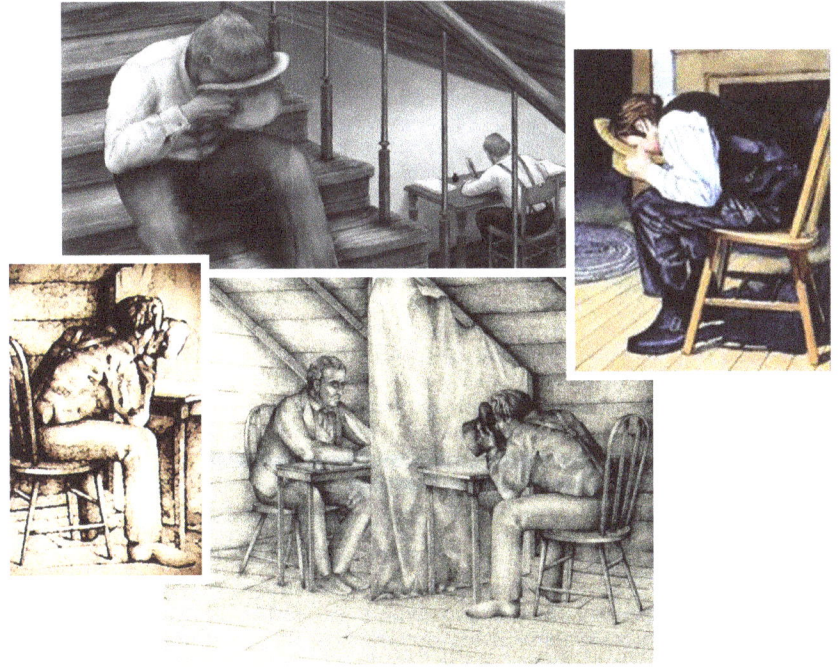

Since learning this disturbing new information and feeling betrayed, I have been attacked and gaslighted by revisionist Mormon apologists claiming that it's my fault and the fault of anyone else for not knowing this. "The information was there all along," they say. "You should've known this," they claim.

Respected LDS historian and scholar Richard Bushman, as quoted above, understands the problem. Unlike these gaslighting revisionist apologists, he has compassion, understanding, and empathy for those who are shocked to learn this faith challenging information.

In 2000, two BYU religion professors, Joseph Fielding McConkie (son of Elder Bruce R. McConkie) and Craig J. Ostler, wrote an essay titled, *"The Process of Translating the Book of Mormon*[9]*."* They wrote:

> *"Thus, everything we have in the Book of Mormon, according to Mr. Whitmer, was translated by placing the chocolate-colored stone in a hat into which Joseph would bury his head so as to close out the light. While doing so he could see 'an oblong piece of parchment, on which the hieroglyphics would appear,' and below the ancient writing, the translation would be given in English. Joseph would then read this to*

> Oliver Cowdery, who in turn would write it. If he did so correctly, the characters and the interpretation would disappear and be replaced by other characters with their interpretation."

After laying the groundwork, the professors continue:

> "Finally, the testimony of David Whitmer simply does not accord with the divine pattern. If Joseph Smith translated everything that is now in the Book of Mormon without using the gold plates, we are left to wonder why the plates were necessary in the first place. It will be remembered that possession of the plates placed the Smith family in considerable danger, causing them a host of difficulties. If the plates were not part of the translation process, this would not have been the case. It also leaves us wondering why the Lord directed the writers of the Book of Mormon to take a duplicate record of the plates of Lehi. This provision which compensated for the loss of the 116 pages would have served no purpose either.
>
> Further, we would be left to wonder why it was necessary for Moroni to instruct Joseph each year for four years before he was entrusted with the plates. We would also wonder why it was so important for Moroni to show the plates to the three witnesses, including David Whitmer. And why did the Lord have the Prophet show the plates to the eight witnesses? Why all this flap and fuss if the Prophet didn't really have the plates and if they were not used in the process of translation?
>
> What David Whitmer is asking us to believe is that the Lord had Moroni seal up the plates and the means by which they were to be translated hundreds of years before they would come into Joseph Smith's possession and then decided to have the Prophet use a seer stone found while digging a well so that none of these things would be necessary after all. Is this, we would ask, really a credible explanation of the way the heavens operate?"

How could it have been expected of me and any other member to know about and to embrace the rock in the hat translation when even these two faithful full-time professors of religion at BYU rejected it as a fictitious lie meant to undermine Joseph Smith and the truth claims of the Restoration?

FIRST VISION
Concerns & Questions

"*Our whole strength rests on the validity of that [first] vision. It either occurred or it did not occur. If it did not, then this work is a fraud. If it did, then it is the most important and wonderful work under the heavens.*"

– PRESIDENT GORDON B. HINCKLEY, *THE MARVELOUS FOUNDATION OF OUR FAITH*[1]

1. There are at least 4 different first vision accounts[2] by Joseph Smith, which the Church admits in its November 2013 *First Vision Accounts* essay:

- 1832 HANDWRITTEN ACCOUNT[3]
- TWO 1835 ACCOUNTS[4]
- 1838 ACCOUNT (OFFICIAL VERSION)[5]
- 1842 ACCOUNT[6]

In the only handwritten account by Joseph Smith, penned in 1832, but not publicly published until much later, describes the first vision in an unfamiliar way:

> "...and while in the attitude of calling upon the Lord in the 16th year of my age a piller of fire light above the brightness of the sun at noon day come down from above and rested upon me and I was filled with the spirit of god and the Lord opened the heavens upon me and I saw the Lord and he spake unto me saying Joseph my son thy sins are forgiven thee. Go thy way walk in my statutes and keep my commandments behold I am the Lord of glory I was crucifyed for the world that all those who believe on my name may have Eternal life..."

- No mention of two beings.
- 12 years after the vision happened.
- Age is 15-years-old ("16th year of my age"), not 14-years-old.
- No reference to asking the question about which church he should join.
- No description of being attacked by Satan.

2. Contradictions: In the 1832 account[7], Joseph wrote that before praying he knew there was no true or living faith or denomination upon the earth as built by Jesus Christ in the New Testament. His primary purpose in going to prayer was to seek forgiveness for his sins.

> "...by searching the scriptures I found that mankind did not come unto the Lord but that they had apostatized from the true and living faith, and there was no society or denomination that was built upon the gospel of Jesus Christ..."

In the official 1838 account[8], however, Joseph wrote:

> "My object in going to inquire of the Lord was to know which of all the sects was right, that I might know which to join"..."(for at this time it had never entered into my heart that all were wrong)."

This is in direct contradiction to his 1832 first vision account.

3. Late appearance of claims: No one - including Joseph Smith's family members and the Saints – had ever heard about the first vision from twelve to twenty-two years after it supposedly occurred. The first and earliest written account of the first vision in Joseph Smith's journal was 12 years after the spring of 1820. There is absolutely no record of any claimed "first vision" prior to this 1832 account.

Despite the emphasis placed on it now, the first vision does not appear to have been widely taught to members of the Church until the 1840s, more than a decade after the Church was founded, and 20 years after it allegedly occurred.

James B. Allen, former BYU Professor and Assistant Church Historian explains [9]:

> "There is little if any evidence, however, that by the early 1830's Joseph Smith was telling the story in public. At least if he were telling it, no one seemed to consider it important enough to have recorded it at the time, and no one was criticizing him for it. Not even in his own history did Joseph Smith mention being criticized in this period for telling the story of the first vision…The fact that none of the available contemporary writings about Joseph Smith in the 1830's, none of the publications of the Church in that decade, and no contemporary journal or correspondence yet discovered mentions the story of the first vision is convincing evidence that at best it received only limited circulation in those early days."

4. Other problems:

- Who appears to him? Depending upon the account, a spirit, an angel, two angels, Jesus, many angels or the Father and the Son appear to him – are all over the place.
- The dates/his ages: The 1832 account states Joseph was 15-years-old while the other accounts state he was 14-years-old when he had the vision.
- The reason or motive for seeking divine help – Bible reading and conviction of sins, a revival, a desire to know if God exists, wanting to know which church to join – are not reported the same in each account.
- Contrary to Joseph's account, the historical record shows that there was no revival in Palmyra, New York in 1820. FairMormon concedes [10]:
  > "While these revivals did not occur in Palmyra itself, their mention in the local newspaper would have given Joseph Smith the sense that there was substantial revival activity in the region."

First Vision

There was one in 1817 and there was another in 1824. There are records from his brother, William Smith, and his mother, Lucy Mack Smith, both stating that the family joined Presbyterianism after Alvin's death [11] in November 1823 despite Joseph Smith claiming in the official 1838 account [12] that they joined in 1820 (3 years before Alvin Smith's death).

- Why did Joseph hold a Trinitarian view of the Godhead, as shown previously with the Book of Mormon, if he clearly saw that the Father and Son were separate embodied beings in the official first vision?

As with the rock in the hat story, I did not know there are multiple first vision accounts. I did not know of their contradictions or that the Church members did not know about a first vision until 12-22 years after it supposedly happened. I was unaware of these omissions in the mission field, as I was never taught or trained in the Missionary Training Center to teach investigators these facts.

BOOK OF ABRAHAM
Concerns & Questions

"None of the characters on the papyrus fragments mentioned Abraham's name or any of the events recorded in the book of Abraham. Mormon and non-Mormon Egyptologists agree that the characters on the fragments do not match the translation given in the book of Abraham, though there is not unanimity, even among non-Mormon scholars, about the proper interpretation of the vignettes on these fragments. Scholars have identified the papyrus fragments as parts of standard funerary texts that were deposited with mummified bodies. These fragments date to between the third century B.C.E. and the first century C.E., long after Abraham lived."

— LDS CHURCH'S *TRANSLATION AND HISTORICITY OF THE BOOK OF ABRAHAM* ESSAY[1]

1. Originally, Joseph claimed that this record was written by Abraham "by his own hand, upon papyrus?" – a claim still prominent in the heading of the Book of Abraham. This claim could not be evaluated for decades as many thought the papyri were lost in a fire. The original papyrus Joseph translated has since been found and, as stated in the Church's July 2014 *Translation and Historicity of the Book of Abraham* [3] essay, "scholars have identified the papyrus fragments as parts of standard funerary texts…[that] date to between the third century B.C.E. and the first century C.E., long after Abraham lived."

We know this is the papyrus that Joseph used for translation because the hieroglyphics match in chronological order to the hieroglyphics in Joseph's *Kirtland Egyptian Papers* [4], which contains his *Grammar & Alphabet of the Egyptian Language* [5] (GAEL). Additionally, the papyrus were pasted onto paper which have drawings of a temple and maps of the Kirtland, Ohio area on the back and they were companied by an affidavit by Emma Smith verifying they had been in the possession of Joseph Smith.

2. Egyptologists have also since translated the source material [6] for the Book of Abraham and have found it to be nothing more than a common pagan Egyptian funerary text for a deceased man named "Hor" around first century C.E. In other words, it was a common Breathing Permit that the Egyptians buried with their dead. It has nothing to do with Abraham or anything Joseph claimed in his translation for the Book of Abraham. The Church admits this in its essay [7]:

> "None of the characters on the papyrus fragments mentioned Abraham's name or any of the events recorded in the book of Abraham. Mormon and non-Mormon Egyptologists agree that the characters on the fragments do not match the translation given in the Book of Abraham, though there is not unanimity, even among non-Mormon scholars, about the proper interpretation of the vignettes on these fragments. Scholars have identified the papyrus fragments as parts of standard funerary texts that were deposited with mummified bodies. These fragments date to between the third century B.C.E. and the first century C.E., long after Abraham lived."

FACSIMILE 1

The graphic below shows the rediscovered papyri placed on top of Facsimile 1. The red circles denote the filled-in sections of facsimile 1 that respected modern Egyptologists say is nonsense.

In contrast with the canonized version of Facsimile 1, the following image is what Facsimile 1 is really supposed to look like, based on Egyptology and the same scene discovered elsewhere in Egypt:

The following is a side-by-side comparison of what Joseph Smith translated in Facsimile 1 and what it actually says, according to Egyptologists and modern Egyptology:

	JOSEPH SMITH'S INTERPRETATION	MODERN EGYPTOLOGICAL INTERPRETATION
1.	The Angel of the Lord	The spirit or "ba" of Hôr (The deceased fellow)
2.	Abraham fastened upon an altar	The deceased: His name was "Hôr"
3.	The idolatrous priest of Elkenah	Anubis. (see original image, this figure was originally portrayed with the head of a Jackal)

44 *Book of Abraham*

4.	The altar for sacrifice by the idolatrous priests, standing before the gods of Elkenah, Libnah, Mahmackrah, Korash, and Pharaoh	A common funeral bier or "lion couch"
5.	The idolatrous god of Elknah	Canopic jars containing the deceased's internal organs. They represent the four sons of the god Horus, who are: #5: Qebehseneuf #6: Duamutef #7: Hapy #8: Imsety
6.	The idolatrous god of Libnah	
7.	The idolatrous god of Mahmackrah	
8.	The idolatrous god of Korash	
9.	The idolatrous god of Pharaoh	This is the god "Horus"
10.	Abraham in Egypt	A libation table bearing wines, oils, etc. Common in Egypt
11.	Designed to represent the pillars of heaven, as understood by Egyptians	A palace facade, called a "serekh"
12.	Raukeeyang, signifying expanse, or the firmament over our heads; but in this case, in relation to this subject, the Egyptians meant it to signify Shaumau, to be hig, or the heavens, answering to the Hebrew word Shaumahyeen	This is just the water that the crocodile swims in

Sources:
Joseph Smith's Translations: Facsimile 1 in Book of Abraham [8]
Modern Egyptological Translations [9]
FairMormon Facsimile 1 Apologetics [10] (notice FairMormon attempts to distract away from line by line translations and instead goes off in irrelevant tangents about sacrifice and other nonsense.)

Figure #3 is supposed to be the jackal-headed Egyptian god of mummification and afterlife, Anubis [11]; not a human. The following images show similar funerary scenes which have been discovered elsewhere in Egypt. Notice that the jackal-headed Egyptian god of death and afterlife Anubis is consistent in every funerary scene.

FACSIMILE 2

The following is a side-by-side comparison of what Joseph Smith translated in Facsimile 2 versus what it actually says according to Egyptologists and modern Egyptology:

	JOSEPH SMITH'S INTERPRETATION	MODERN EGYPTOLOGICAL INTERPRETATION
1.	Kolob, The residence of God	The god Khnumu
2.	Stands next to Kolob, called by the Egyptians Oliblish…	"Amun-Re", god with two faces representing rising & setting sun
3.	God sitting on his throne, clothed with power and authority	"Horus-Re" riding in his boat
4.	Raukeeyang; also the number 1000; The measuring of time of Oliblish	Represents Sokar, not a number
5.	Enish-go-on-dosh; a governing planet	Cow of Hathor behind which stand a uzat-headed goddess holding a sacred tree
6.	Represents this earth in its four quarters	The four sons of Horus, they can represent the four cardinal points of earth
7.	God sitting on his throne, revealing through the heavens the grand Key-words of the priesthood	The god "Min", an ithyphallic god; that is, a sexually aroused male deity
8.	Contains writings that can only be revealed in the temple	"grant that the souls of Osiris Shechonk may live"
9.	Ought not to be revealed at the present time	"the netherworld (below the earth) and his great waters.

Book of Abraham

10.	Ought not to be revealed at the present time	*Oh might god, lord of heaven and earth*
11.		*O god of the sleeping ones from the time of creation (read in order 11,10,9,8)*
12.		*"near" and "wrap"*
13.		*"which made by"*
14.		*"breathings"*
15.		*"this book"*
16.	Will be given in the own due time of the Lord	*"and may this soul and its posessor never be decreased in the netherworld"*
17.		*"may this tomb never be desecrated"*
18.		*"I am Djabty in the house of Benben in Heliopolis, so exalted and glorious. (I am) copulating bull without equal. (I am) that mighty god in the house of Benben of Heliopolis... that might god..."*
19. 20. 21.		"You shall be as that God, the Busirian"
22.	No Annotation Given	"The name of this mighty god"
23.		*Baboons are adoring the souls of that realm*

Sources:
Joseph Smith's Translations: Facsimile 2 in Book of Abraham.[12]
Modern Egyptological Translations.[13]
FairMormon Facsimile 2 Apologetics.[14] *(Joseph may have gotten 1 out of 21 translations correct!)*

One of the most disturbing facts I discovered in my research of Facsimile 2 is figure #7. Joseph Smith said that this is "God sitting on his throne…" It's actually Min,[15] the pagan Egyptian god of fertility or sex. Min is sitting on a throne with an erect penis (which can be seen in the figure). In other words, Joseph interpreted that this figure with an erect penis is Heavenly Father sitting on His throne.

FACSIMILE 3

The following is a side-by-side comparison of what Joseph Smith translated in Facsimile 3 versus what it actually says according to Egyptologists and modern Egyptology:

	JOSEPH SMITH'S INTERPRETATION	MODERN EGYPTOLOGICAL INTERPRETATION
1.	*Abraham sitting on Pharaoh's throne, by the politeness of the king, with a crown upon his head, representing the priesthood, as emblematical of the grand Presidency in heaven; with the scepter of justice and judgment in his hand*	*This is Osiris. Writing above figure: "Recitation by Osiris, Foremost of the Westerners." The "atef" crown also identifies him as Osiris*

Book of Abraham **49**

2.	King Pharaoh, whose name is given in the characters above his head		This figure is female, not male. Writing above figure: "Isis the great, the god's mother"
3.	Signifies Abraham in Egypt as given also in Figure 10 of Facsimile No. 1.		This is a libation table (wine, oils, etc.)
4.	Prince of Pharaoh, King of Egypt, as written above the hand		This figure is female, not male. Writing above figure: "Maat, mistress of the gods"
5.	Shulem, one of the kings principal waiters, as represented by the characters above his hand		This is a deceased individual wearing the traditional cone of perfumed grease and lotus flower on his head. Writing above figure: "The Osiris Hor, justified forever"
6.	Olimlah, a slave belonging to the prince		Not a slave. This is Anubis, guide of the dead, who is there to support the deceased. Writing above figure: "Recitation by Anubis, who makes protection(?), foremost of the embalming booth,..."

Sources:
Joseph Smith's Translations: Facsimile 3 in Book of Abraham [16]
Modern Egyptological Translations [17]
FairMormon Facsimile 3 Apologetics [18] ("There are LDS experts who believe the Book of Abraham is a genuine artifact, and that it testifies of Joseph Smith's status as a prophet. Non-LDS experts obviously do not agree with that.")

3. Respected non-LDS Egyptologists state that Joseph Smith's translation of the papyri and facsimiles are gibberish and have absolutely nothing to do with the papyri and facsimiles and what they actually say.

FACSIMILE 1

1. The names are wrong.
2. The Abraham scene is wrong.
3. He names gods that are not part of the Egyptian belief system; of any known mythology or belief system.

FACSIMILE 2

1. Joseph translated 11 figures on this facsimile. None of the names are correct and none of the gods exist in Egyptian religion or any recorded mythology.
2. Joseph misidentifies every god in this facsimile.

FACSIMILE 3

1. Joseph misidentifies the Egyptian god Osiris[19] as Abraham.
2. Misidentifies the Egyptian god Isis[20] as the Pharaoh.
3. Misidentifies the Egyptian god Maat[21] as the Prince of the Pharaoh.
4. Misidentifies the Egyptian god Anubis[11] as a slave.
5. Misidentifies the dead Hor as a waiter.
6. Joseph misidentifies – twice – a female as a male.

4. The Book of Abraham teaches an incorrect Newtonian view of the universe[22]. These Newtonian astronomical concepts, mechanics, and models of the universe have since been succeeded and substantially modified by 20th century Einsteinian physics.

What we find in Abraham 3 and the official scriptures of the LDS Church regarding science reflects a Newtonian world concept. Just as the Catholic Church's Ptolemaic cosmology was displaced by the new Copernican and Newtonian world model, however, the nineteenth-century, canonized, Newtonian world view has since been displaced by Einstein's twentieth-century science.

Keith E. Norman, an LDS scholar[23], has written that for the LDS Church:

> *"It is no longer possible to pretend there is no conflict."*

Norman continues:

> "Scientific cosmology began its leap forward just when Mormon doctrine was becoming stabilized. The revolution in twentieth-century physics precipitated by Einstein dethroned Newtonian physics as the ultimate explanation of the way the universe works. Relativity theory and quantum mechanics, combined with advances in astronomy, have established a vastly different picture of how the universe began, how it is structured and operates, and the nature of matter and energy. This new scientific cosmology poses a serious challenge to the Mormon version of the universe."

Grant Palmer, a Mormon historian and CES teacher for 34 years, wrote:

> "Many of the astronomical and cosmological ideas found in both Joseph Smith's environment and in the Book of Abraham have become out of vogue, and some of these Newtonian concepts are scientific relics. The evidence suggests that the Book of Abraham reflects concepts of Joseph Smith's time and place rather than those of an ancient world."
> – An Insider's View of Mormon Origins, p.25 [24]

5. 86% of Book of Abraham chapters 2, 4, and 5 are King James Version Genesis chapters 1, 2, 11, and 12. Sixty-six out of seventy-seven verses are quotations or close paraphrases of King James Version wording. (See An Insider's View of Mormon Origins, p.19) [25]

If the Book of Abraham is an ancient text written thousands of years ago "by his own hand upon papyrus," then what are 17th century King James Version text doing in there? What does this say about the book being anciently written by Abraham?

6. Why are there anachronisms in the Book of Abraham? For example, the terms *Chaldeans*, *Egyptus*, and *Pharaoh* are all anachronistic [26]. Additionally, Abraham refers to the facsimiles in 1:12 [27] and 1:14 [28]. However, as noted and conceded above in the Church's essay, these facsimiles did not even exist in Abraham's time as they are standard first century C.E. pagan Egyptian funerary documents.

> "Some have assumed that the hieroglyphs adjacent to and surrounding facsimile 1 must be a source for the text of the book of Abraham."
> – Translation and Historicity of the Book of Abraham essay, lds.org

WHY WOULD ANYONE ASSUME THAT?

> *"And it came to pass that the priests laid violence upon me, that they might slay me also, as they did those virgins upon this altar; and that you may have a knowledge of this altar, I will refer you to the representation at the commencement of this record."*
> – Abraham 1:12

7. Facsimile 2, Figure #5 states the sun receives its "light from the revolutions of Kolob." We now know, however, that the process of nuclear fusion is what makes the stars and suns shine. With the discovery of quantum mechanics, scientists learned that the sun's source of energy is internal and not external. The sun shines because of thermonuclear fusion. The sun does not shine because it gets its light from any other star or any other external source.

8. There is a book published in 1829 by Thomas Dick entitled *The Philosophy of a Future State*[29]. Joseph Smith owned a copy[30] of the book and Oliver Cowdery quoted some lengthy excerpts from the book in the December 1836 *Messenger and Advocate*[31]. Klaus Hansen, an LDS scholar, stated:

> *"The progressive aspect of Joseph's theology, as well as its cosmology, while in a general way compatible with antebellum thought, bears some remarkable resemblances to Thomas Dick's 'Philosophy of a Future State'."*

Hansen continues:

> *"Some very striking parallels to Smith's theology suggest that the similarities between the two may be more than coincidental. Dick's lengthy book, an ambitious treatise on astronomy and metaphysics, proposed the idea that matter is eternal and indestructible and rejected the notion of a creation ex nihilo. Much of the book dealt with the infinity of the universe, made up of innumerable stars spread out over immeasurable distances. Dick speculated that many of these stars were peopled by 'various orders of intelligences' and that these intelligences were 'progressive beings' in various stages of evolution toward perfection. In the Book of Abraham, part of which consists of a treatise on astronomy and cosmology, eternal beings of various orders and stages of development likewise populate numerous stars. They, too, are called 'intelligences.' Dick speculated that 'the systems of the universe revolve around a common centre…the throne of God.' In the Book of Abraham, one star named Kolob 'was nearest unto the throne of God.' Other stars, in ever diminishing order,*

were placed in increasing distances from this center."
– Mormonism and the American Experience, p.79-80, 110 [32]

9. Elder Jeffrey R. Holland was directly asked about the papyri not matching the Book of Abraham in a March 2012 BBC interview [33]:

> **Sweeney:** *"Mr. Smith got this papyri and he translated them and subsequently as the Egyptologists cracked the code something completely different..."*
>
> **Holland:** *"(Interrupts) All I'm saying...all I'm saying is that what got translated got translated into the word of God. The vehicle for that, I do not understand and don't claim to know and know no Egyptian."*

Is "I don't know and I don't understand but it's the word of God" really the best answer that a "prophet, seer, and revelator" can come up with to such a profound problem and stumbling block that is driving many members out of the Church?

The following are respected Egyptian scholars/Egyptologists statements regarding Joseph Smith and the Book of Abraham:

> *"...these three facsimiles of Egyptian documents in the Pearl of Great Price depict the most common objects in the Mortuary religion of Egypt. Joseph Smith's interpretations of them as part of a unique revelation through Abraham, therefore, very clearly demonstrates that he was totally unacquainted with the significance of these documents and absolutely ignorant of the simplest facts of Egyptian writing and civilization."*
> – Dr. James H. Breasted, University of Chicago, Joseph Smith, Jr., As a Translator, p.26-27 [34]

> *"It may be safely said that there is not one single word that is true in these explanations."*
> – Dr. W.M. Flinders Petrie, London University, Joseph Smith, Jr., As a Translator, p.24 [35]

> *"It is difficult to deal seriously with Joseph Smith's impudent fraud... Smith has turned the goddess [Isis in Facsimile #3] into a king and Osiris into Abraham."*
> – Dr. A.H. Sayce, Oxford professor of Egyptology, Joseph Smith, Jr., As a Translator, p.23 [36]

In addition to the above, world renowned and respected University of Chicago professor of Egyptology, Dr. Robert Ritner, provided a detailed response and rebuttal to the LDS Church's *Translation and Historicity of the Book of Abraham*[37] essay that is sobering and devastating. Dr. Ritner's rebuttal to the Church's essay can be read here[38].

The following video[39] offers a thorough, complete, and unbiased overview of the Book of Abraham issues as well as the apologetic responses to them:

CESLETTER.ORG/PAPYRI

An online contributor created an easy-to-understand document[40] very clearly outlining the Book of Abraham issues. Contrary to what some Mormon apologists claim or imply, a person does not have to be an Egyptologist or a scholar with a PhD to clearly understand the Book of Abraham problems and challenges to Joseph Smith's claims of being a translator.

Of all the issues, the Book of Abraham is the issue that has both fascinated and disturbed me the most. It is the issue that I've spent the most time researching because it offers a real insight into Joseph's modus operandi as well as Joseph's claim of being a translator. It is the smoking gun that has completely obliterated my testimony of Joseph Smith and his claims.

POLYGAMY | POLYANDRY
Concerns & Questions

"So, the question of Polyandry. Polygamy is when a man has multiple wives. Polyandry is when a man marries another man's wife. Joseph did both."

– ELDER MARLIN K. JENSEN, LDS CHURCH HISTORIAN
SWEDISH RESCUE FIRESIDE[1] | AUDIO[2]

One of the things that also truly disturbed me in my research was discovering the real origins of polygamy and how Joseph Smith really practiced it.

- Joseph Smith was married to at least 34 women[3], as now verified in the Church's 2014 polygamy essays.

- Polyandry[4]: Of those 34 women, 11 of them were married women of other living men. Among them being Apostle Orson Hyde, who was sent on his mission to dedicate Palestine when Joseph secretly married his wife, Marinda Hyde[5]. Church Historian Elder Marlin K. Jensen[6] and unofficial apologists like FairMormon[7] do not dispute the polyandry.

UPDATE: The Church admits the polyandry in its October 2014 *Plural Marriage in Kirtland and Nauvoo*[8] essay.

The Church and apologists now attempt to justify these polyandrous marriages by theorizing that they probably didn't include sexual relations and thus were "eternal" or "dynastic" sealings only. How is not having sex with a living man's wife on earth only to take her away from him in the eternities to be one of your [Joseph] forty wives any better or any less immoral?

During the summer of 1841, Joseph Smith tested Helen Mar Kimball's father, Apostle Heber C. Kimball, by asking Heber to give his wife, Vilate – Helen's mother – to Joseph:

> "…*shortly after Heber's return from England, he was introduced to the doctrine of plural marriage directly through a startling test — a sacrifice that shook his very being and challenged his faith to the ultimate. He had already sacrificed homes, possessions, friends, relatives, all worldly rewards, peace, and tranquility for the Restoration. Nothing was left to place on the altar save his life, his children, and his wife. Then came the Abrahamic test. Joseph demanded for himself what to Heber was the unthinkable, his Vilate. Totally crushed spiritually and emotionally, Heber touched neither food nor water for three days and three nights and continually sought confirmation and comfort from God. On the evening of the third day, some kind of assurance came, and Heber took Vilate to the upper room of Joseph's store on Water Street. The Prophet wept at this act of faith, devotion, and obedience. Joseph had never*

intended to take Vilate. It was all a test."

— Heber C. Kimball: Mormon Patriarch and Pioneer, p.93.[9]

If Joseph's polygamous/polyandrous marriages are innocuous "dynastic sealings" meant for the afterlife, as the Church and apologists are now theorizing, and Joseph wanted to "dynastically link" himself to the Kimball family, why was Apostle Heber C. Kimball so troubled by Joseph's command for his wife that he "touched neither food nor water for three days and three nights"?

- Out of the 34 women, 7 of them were teenage girls as young as 14-years-old. Joseph was 37-years-old when he married 14-year-old Helen Mar Kimball[10], twenty-three years his junior. Even by 19th century standards, this is shocking.

UPDATE: The Church now admits that Joseph Smith married Helen Mar Kimball "several months before her 15th birthday" in its October 2014 Plural Marriage in Kirtland and Nauvoo[11] essay.

Joseph took 14-year-old Helen Mar Kimball's hand in marriage after his disturbing Abrahamic test on her father, Heber, while promising Helen and her family eternal salvation and exaltation if she accepted:

> *"Just previous to my father's starting upon his last mission but one, to the Eastern States, he taught me the principle of Celestial marriage, and having a great desire to be connected with the Prophet Joseph, he offered me to him; this I afterwards learned from the Prophet's own mouth. My father had but one Ewe lamb, but willingly laid her upon the alter: how cruel this seemed to the mother whose heartstrings were already stretched until they were ready to snap asunder, for he had taken Sarah Noon to wife and she thought she had made sufficient sacrifice, but the Lord required more. I will pass over the temptations which I had during the twenty four hours after my father introduced to me the principle and asked me if I would be sealed to Joseph, who came next morning and with my parents I heard him teach and explain the principle of Celestial marriage - after which he said to me, 'If you will take this step, it will ensure your eternal salvation and exaltation and that of your father's household and all of your kindred.'"*
>
> *This promise was so great that I willingly gave myself to purchase so glorious a reward. None but God and angels could see my*

> *mother's bleeding heart – when Joseph asked her if she was willing, she replied, 'If Helen is willing, I have nothing more to say.' She had witnessed the sufferings of others, who were older and who better understood the step they were taking, and to see her child, who had scarcely seen her fifteenth summer, following in the same thorny path, in her mind she saw the misery which was as sure to come as the sun was to rise and set; but it was all hidden from me."*
>
> – Helen Mar Kimball Whitney 1881 Autobiography, A Woman's View, BYU Religious Studies Center, 1997, p.482-487 [12]

Why all the agony and anguish if this was an innocuous "Dynastic Linking" and sealing for the afterlife? Why did it seem "cruel" to Vilate, "whose heartstrings were already stretched"?

- Among the women and girls was a mother-daughter set and three sister sets [13]. Several of these girls included Joseph's own foster daughters who lived and worked in the Smith home (Lawrence sisters [14], Partridge sisters [15], Lucy Walker [16]).

If some of these marriages were non-sexual "dynastic" "eternal" sealings only, as theorized by the Church and apologists, why would Joseph need to be sealed to a mother and daughter set? The mother would be sealed to the daughter and would become part of Joseph's afterlife family through the sealing to her mother.

Further, Joseph died without being sealed to his children or to his parents [17]. If a primary motive of these "sealings" was to be connected in the afterlife, as claimed by the Church and apologists, what does it say about Joseph's priorities and motives to be sealed to a non-related and already married woman (Patty Sessions [18]) and her 23-year-old already married daughter (Sylvia Sessions [19]) than it was to be sealed to his own parents and to his own children?

- Joseph was married/sealed to at least 22 other women and girls before finally being sealed to his first legal wife, Emma, on May 28, 1843 [20]. Emma was not aware of most of these other girls/women and their marriages to her husband. Why was "elect lady [21]" Emma the 23rd wife to be sealed to Joseph?

Some of the marriages to these women included promises by Joseph of eternal life to the girls and their families, or threats that he (Joseph) was going to be slain by an angel with a drawn sword [22] if the girls didn't marry him.

I have a problem with this. This is Warren Jeffs [23] territory. This is not the Joseph Smith I grew up learning about in the Church and having a testimony of. This is not the Joseph Smith to whom I sang "Praise to the Man" or taught others about for two years in the mission field.

Many members do not realize that there is a set of very specific and bizarre rules outlined in Doctrine & Covenants 132 [24] (still in LDS canon despite President Hinckley publicly stating that polygamy is not doctrinal [25]) on how polygamy is to be practiced. It is the kind of revelation you would expect from the likes of Warren Jeffs to his FLDS followers.

The only form of polygamy permitted by D&C 132 is a union with a virgin after first giving the opportunity to the first wife to consent to the marriage. If the first wife doesn't consent, the husband is exempt and may still take an additional wife, but the first wife must at least have the opportunity to consent. In case the first wife doesn't consent, she will be "destroyed." Also, the new wife must be a virgin before the marriage and be completely monogamous after the marriage or she will be destroyed (D&C 132:41 [26] & 63 [27]). It is interesting that the only prerequisite that is mentioned for the man is that he must desire another wife: "if any man espouse a virgin, and desire to espouse another…[28]" It does not say that the man must get a specific revelation from the living prophet, although many members today assume that this is how polygamy was practiced.

D&C 132 is unequivocal on the point that polygamy is permitted only "to multiply and replenish the earth" and "bear the souls of men." This would be consistent with the Book of Mormon prohibition on polygamy except in the case where God commands it to "raise up seed [29]."

AGAIN, CONTRARY TO D&C 132, THE FOLLOWING SUMMARIZES HOW POLYGAMY WAS ACTUALLY PRACTICED BY JOSEPH SMITH

- Joseph married 11 women who were already married. Multiple husbands = Polyandry [30].
- Unions without the knowledge or consent of the husband, in cases of polyandry.
- These married women continued to live as husband and wife with their first husband after marrying Joseph.
- A union with Apostle Orson Hyde's wife while he was on a mission (Marinda Hyde [31]).

- A union with a newlywed and pregnant woman (Zina Huntington [32]).

- Threats that Joseph would be slain by an angel with a drawn sword if they did not enter into the union (Zina Huntington, Almera Woodard Johnson, Mary Lightner [33]).

- Unions without the knowledge or consent of first wife Emma, including to teenagers who worked with Emma in the Smith home such as the Partridge sisters and the Lawrence girls.

- Promises of salvation and exaltation for the girls and/or their entire families.

JOSEPH'S POLYGAMY ALSO INCLUDED:

- Dishonesty in public sermons, 1835 D&C 101:4 [34], denials by Joseph Smith that he was practicing polygamy, Joseph's destruction of the *Nauvoo Expositor* [35] that exposed his polygamy and which destruction of the printing press initiated the chain of events that led to Joseph's death.

- An illegal marriage to Fanny Alger [36], which was described by Oliver Cowdery as a "dirty, nasty, filthy affair [37]" – *Rough Stone Rolling*, p.323

William McLellin reported a conversation he had with Emma Smith in 1847, which account [38] is accepted by both LDS and non-LDS historians, describing how Emma discovered her husband's affair with Fanny Alger:

> "One night she [Emma] missed Joseph and Fanny Alger. She went to the barn and saw him and Fanny in the barn together alone. She looked through a crack and saw the transaction!!! She told me this story too was verily true."

LDS polygamy apologists further discuss Emma's disturbing discovery and the aftermath here [39].

- Joseph was practicing polygamy before the sealing authority was given. LDS historian, Richard Bushman, states: "There is evidence that Joseph was a polygamist by 1835" – *Rough Stone Rolling*, p.323 [40]. Plural marriages are rooted in the notion of "sealing" for both time and eternity. The "sealing" power was not restored until April 3, 1836 when Elijah appeared to Joseph in the Kirtland Temple [41] and conferred the sealing keys upon him. So, Joseph's "marriage" to

Fanny Alger in 1833 was illegal under both the laws of the land and under any theory of divine authority; it was adultery.

D&C 132:63 [42] very clearly states that the only purpose of polygamy is to "multiply and replenish the earth" and "bear the souls of men." Why did Joseph marry women who were already married? These women were obviously not virgins, which violated D&C 132:61 [43]. Zina Huntington had been married seven and a half months and was about six months pregnant with her first husband's baby at the time she married Joseph; clearly she didn't need any more help to "bear the souls of men."

How about the consent of the first wife, which receives so much attention in D&C 132? Emma was unaware of most of Joseph's plural marriages, at least until after the fact, which violated D&C 132.

The secrecy of the marriages and the private and public denials by Joseph Smith are not congruent with honest behavior. Emma was not informed of most of these marriages until after the fact. The Saints did not know what was going on behind the scenes as polygamy did not become common knowledge until 1852 when Brigham Young revealed it in Utah. Joseph Smith did everything he could to keep the practice secret from the Church and the public. In fact, Joseph's desire to keep this part of his life a secret is what ultimately contributed to his death when he ordered the destruction of the *Nauvoo Expositor*, which dared publicly expose his private behavior in June 1844. This event initiated a chain of events that ultimately led to his death at the Carthage jail.

Consider the following denial made by Joseph Smith to Latter-day Saints in Nauvoo in May 1844 – a mere few weeks before his death:

> "...What a thing it is for a man to be accused of committing adultery, and having seven wives, when I can only find one. I am the same man, and as innocent as I was fourteen years ago; and I can prove them all perjurers."
> – *History of the Church, Vol. 6, Chapter 19, p.411* [44]

It is a matter of historical fact that Joseph had secretly taken over 30 plural wives by May 1844 when he made the above denial that he was ever a polygamist.

If you go to FamilySearch.org [45] – an LDS-owned genealogy website – you can clearly see that Joseph Smith had many wives (click to expand on Joseph's wives). The Church's October 2014 *Plural Marriage in Kirtland and Nauvoo* [46] essay acknowledges that Joseph Smith was a polygamist. The facts speak for themselves – from 100% LDS sources – that Joseph Smith was dishonest.

The following 1835 edition of Doctrine & Covenants revelations bans polygamy:

1835 DOCTRINE & COVENANTS 101:4 [47]

"Inasmuch as this Church of Christ has been reproached with the crime of fornication, and polygamy: we declare that we believe, that one man should have one wife; and one woman, but one husband, except in case of death, when either is at liberty to marry again."

1835 DOCTRINE & COVENANTS 13:7 [48]

"Thou shalt love thy wife with all thy heart, and shall cleave unto her and none else."

1835 DOCTRINE & COVENANTS 65:3 [49]

"Wherefore, it is lawful that he should have one wife, and they twain shall be one flesh, and all this that the earth might answer the end of its creation."

Joseph Smith was already a polygamist when these revelations were introduced into the 1835 edition of the Doctrine & Covenants [50] and Joseph publicly taught that the doctrine of the Church was monogamy. Nevertheless, Joseph continued secretly marrying multiple women and girls as these revelations/scriptures remained in force.

In an attempt to influence and abate public rumors of his secret polygamy, Joseph asked 31 witnesses to sign an affidavit published in the LDS October 1, 1842 *Times and Seasons* [51] stating that Joseph did not practice polygamy. Pointing to the above-mentioned D&C 101:4 scripture, these witnesses claimed the following:

"…we know of no other rule or system of marriage than the one published from the Book of Doctrine and Covenants."

The problem with this affidavit is that it was signed by several people who were secret polygamists or who knew that Joseph was a polygamist at the time they signed the affidavit. In fact, Eliza R. Snow [52], one of the signers of this affidavit, was Joseph Smith's plural wife. Joseph and Eliza had been married 3 months earlier, on June 29, 1842. Two Apostles and future prophets, John Taylor and Wilford Woodruff, were also aware of Joseph's polygamy behind the scenes when they signed the affidavit. Another signer, Bishop Whitney, had personally married his daughter Sarah Ann Whitney [53] to Joseph as a plural wife a few months earlier on July 27, 1842. Whitney's wife and Sarah's mother Elizabeth (also a signer) witnessed the ceremony.

What does it say about Joseph Smith and his character to include his plural wife and associates – who knew about his secret polygamy/polyandry – to lie and perjure in a sworn public affidavit that Joseph was not a polygamist?

Now, does the fact that Joseph Smith practiced polygamy and polyandry while denying and lying to Emma, the Saints, and the world over the course of 10+ years of his life prove that he was a false prophet? That the Church is false? No, it doesn't.

What it does prove, however, is that Joseph Smith's pattern of behavior or modus operandi for a period of at least 10 years of his adult life was to keep secrets, to be deceptive, and to be dishonest – both privately and publicly.

It's when you take this snapshot of Joseph's character and start looking into the Book of Abraham, the Kinderhook Plates, the Book of Mormon, the multiple First Vision accounts, Priesthood Restoration, and so on that you begin to see a *very* disturbing pattern and picture.

Today, Warren Jeffs is more closely aligned to Joseph Smith's Mormonism than the modern LDS Church is.

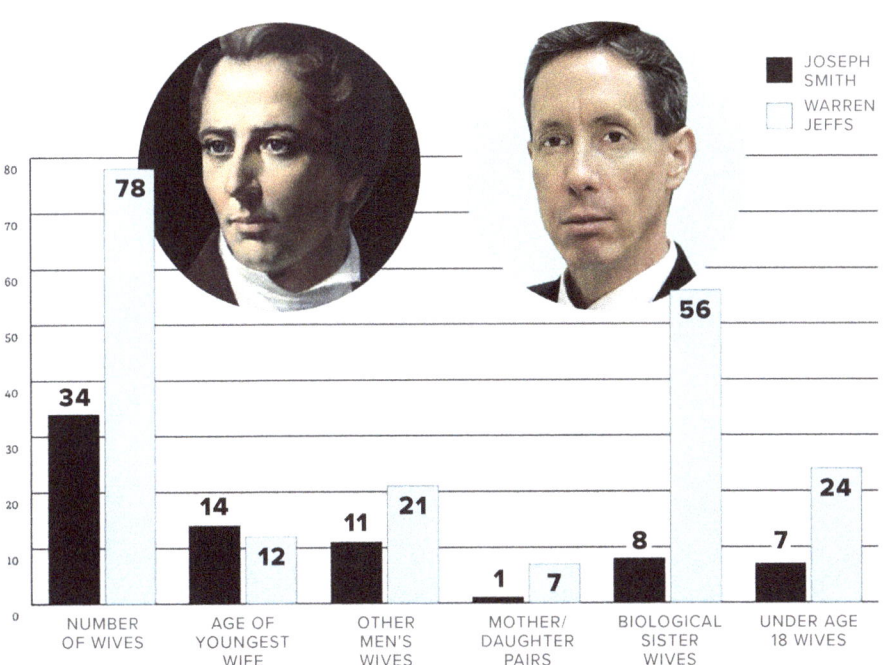

Sources: cesletter.org/polygamy/54

JOSEPH SMITH'S POLYGAMY | POLYANDRY

JOSEPH SMITH, JR.

EMMA SMITH[1] — Joseph and Emma married in Jan. 1827

Eliza, like many of the wives, went on to marry Brigham Young.

Wife #2	FANNY ALGER	Age 16 (Lived in Smith home as housekeeper)
Wife #16	SARAH ANN WHITNEY	Age 17
Wife #19	FLORA ANN WOODWORTH	Age 16
Wife #4	LOUISA BEAMAN	
Wife #7	AGNES COOLBRITH	
Wife #3	LUCINDA MORGAN HARRIS	— GEORGE W. HARRIS
Wife #5	ZINA HUNTINGTON JACOBS	— HENRY JACOBS
Wife #6	PRESENDIA HUNTINGTON BUELL	— NORMAN BUELL
Wife #24	SARAH LAWRENCE	Age 17
Wife #25	MARIA LAWRENCE	
Wife #30	DESDEMONA FULMER	
Wife #10	PATTY BARTLETT SESSIONS	— DAVID SESSIONS
Wife #8	SYLVIA SESSIONS LYON	— WINDSOR LYON
Wife #23	LUCY WALKER	Age 17
Wife #14	DELEENA JOHNSON	
Wife #15	ELIZA R. SNOW	
Wife #26	HELEN MAR KIMBALL	Age 14 (The youngest of the child brides)
Wife #20	EMILY DOW PARTRIDGE	
Wife #21	ELIZA MARIA PARTRIDGE	
	MARY ROLLINS LIGHTNER[9]	— ADAM LIGHTNER
Wife #33	NANCY WINCHESTER	Age 15
Wife #17	MARTHA MCBRIDE KNIGHT	
Wife #22	ALMERA JOHNSON	
Wife #13	SARAH KINGSLEY CLEVELAND	— JOHN CLEVELAND
Wife #31	OLIVE FROST	
Wife #32	MELISSA LOTT	
Wife #27	HANNA ELLS	
	ORSON HYDE — MARINDA JOHNSON HYDE (Wife #11)	
Wife #18	RUTH VOSE SAYERS	— EDWARD SAYERS
Wife #34	FANNY YOUNG	
Wife #29	RHODA RICHARDS	
	JABEZ DURFEE — ELIZABETH DAVIS DURFEE (Wife #12)	
Wife #28	ELVIRA COWLES HOLMES	— JONATHON HOLMES

Legend:
- WIVES UNDER AGE 18
- OTHER POLYGAMOUS WIVES
- POLYANDROUS MARRIAGES
- CONCURRENT LIVING HUSBANDS
- SISTERS
- MOTHER & DAUGHTER
- SENT AWAY BY JOSEPH TO SERVE A MISSION

Sources: cesletter.org/polygamy/55

PROPHETS
Concerns & Questions

"…The Lord will never permit me or any other man who stands as President of the Church to lead you astray. It is not in the program. It is not in the mind of God. If I were to attempt that, the Lord would remove me out of my place."

– PRESIDENT WILFORD WOODRUFF, *WILFORD WOODRUFF: HISTORY OF HIS LIFE AND LABORS*, P.572[1]

"Keep the eyes of the mission on the leaders of the Church…We will not and…cannot lead [you] astray."

– ELDER M. RUSSELL BALLARD, *STAY IN THE BOAT AND HOLD ON!*[2], OCTOBER 2014 CONFERENCE

"Today, the Church disavows the theories advanced in the past that black skin is a sign of divine disfavor or curse, or that it reflects unrighteous actions in a premortal life…"

– *2013 RACE AND THE PRIESTHOOD*[3] ESSAY, LDS.ORG

(2013 "Prophets, Seers, and Revelators" throwing yesterday's "Prophets, Seers, and Revelators" under the bus over yesterday's racist revelations and doctrines)

1. ADAM-GOD

President Brigham Young taught what is now known as "Adam–God theory [4]." He taught that Adam is "our Father and our God, and the only God with whom we have to do." Brigham not only taught this doctrine over the pulpit in conferences in 1852 [5] and 1854 [6] but he also introduced this doctrine as the Lecture at the Veil [7] in the endowment ceremony of the Temple.

Brigham also published this doctrine in the *Deseret News* on June 18, 1873 [8]:

> "*How much unbelief exists in the minds of the Latter-day Saints in regard to one particular* **doctrine which I revealed to them, and which God revealed to me – namely that Adam is our father and God** *– I do not know, I do not inquire, I care nothing about it. Our Father Adam helped to make this earth, it was created expressly for him, and after it was made he and his companions came here. He brought one of his wives with him, and she was called Eve, because she was the first woman upon the earth.* **Our Father Adam is the man who stands at the gate and holds the keys of everlasting life and salvation to all his children who have or who ever will come upon the earth**. *I have been found fault with by the ministers of religion because I have said that they were ignorant. But I could not find any man on the earth who could tell me this, although it is one of the simplest things in the world, until I met and talked with Joseph Smith.*"

Contrary to the teachings of Brigham Young, subsequent prophets and apostles have since renounced the Adam-God theory as false doctrine. President Spencer W. Kimball renounced the Adam-God theory in the October 1976 General Conference:

> "*We warn you against the dissemination of doctrines which are not according to the scriptures and which are alleged to have been taught by some of the General Authorities of past generations. Such, for instance, is the Adam-God theory. We denounce that theory and hope that everyone will be cautioned against this and other kinds of false doctrine.*"
>
> – *Our Own Liahona* [9]

Along with President Spencer W. Kimball and similar statements from others, Elder Bruce R. McConkie made the following statement:

> "*The devil keeps this heresy [Adam-God theory] alive as a means of obtaining converts to cultism. It is contrary to the whole plan of salvation set forth in the scriptures, and anyone who has read the Book of Moses, and anyone who has received the temple endowment, has no excuse whatever for being led astray by it. Those who are so ensnared reject the*

living prophet and close their ears to the apostles of their day."
— *The Seven Deadly Heresies* [10]

Ironically, Elder McConkie's June 1980 condemnation asks you to trust him and President Kimball as today's living prophet. Further, McConkie is pointing to the endowment ceremony as a source of factual information. What about the Saints of Brigham's day who were following their living prophet? And what about the endowment ceremony of their day where Adam-God was being taught at the veil?

Yesterday's doctrine is today's false doctrine and yesterday's prophet is today's heretic.

2. BLOOD ATONEMENT

Along with Adam-God, Brigham taught a doctrine known as "Blood Atonement [11]" where a person's blood had to be shed to atone for their own sins as it was beyond the atonement of Jesus Christ.

> *"There are sins that men commit for which they cannot receive forgiveness in this world, or in that which is to come, and if they had their eyes open to see their true condition, they would be perfectly willing to have their blood spilt upon the ground, that the smoke thereof might ascend to heaven as an offering for their sins; and the smoking incense would atone for their sins, whereas, if such is not the case, they will stick to them and remain upon them in the spirit world.*
>
> *I know, when you hear my brethren telling about cutting people off from the earth, that you consider it is strong doctrine; but it is to save them, not to destroy them…*
>
> *And furthermore, I know that there are transgressors, who, if they knew themselves, and the only condition upon which they can obtain forgiveness, would beg of their brethren to shed their blood, that the smoke thereof might ascend to God as an offering to appease the wrath that is kindled against them, and that the law might have its course. I will say further;*
>
> *I have had men come to me and offer their lives to atone for their sins. It is true that the blood of the Son of God was shed for sins through the fall and those committed by men, yet men can commit sins which it can never remit…There are sins that can be atoned for by an offering upon an altar, as in ancient days; and there are sins that the blood of a lamb, or a calf, or of turtle dove, cannot remit, but they must be atoned for by the blood of the man."*
>
> — *Journal of Discourses* 4:53-54 [12]

UPDATE: The Church now confirms in its *Peace and Violence among 19th-Century Latter-day Saints* [13] essay that Blood Atonement was taught by the prophet Brigham Young.

As with the Adam-God theory, the Blood Atonement doctrine was later declared false by subsequent prophets and apostles.

Yesterday's doctrine is today's false doctrine. Yesterday's prophet is today's heretic.

3. POLYGAMY

Brigham Young taught the doctrine that polygamy is required for exaltation:

> "The only men who become Gods, even the Sons of God, are those who enter into polygamy."
> — *Journal of Discourses* 11:269 [14]

Several other prophets after Young, including Taylor, Woodruff, Snow, and Joseph F. Smith gave similar teachings that the New and Everlasting Covenant of plural marriage was doctrinal and essential for exaltation.

It's even in the scriptures:

> **DOCTRINE & COVENANTS 132:4** [15]
> "For behold, I reveal unto you a new and an everlasting covenant; and if ye abide not that covenant, then are ye damned; for no one can reject this covenant and be permitted to enter into my glory."

In a September 1998 *Larry King Live* interview [16], President Hinckley was asked about polygamy:

> **Larry King:** *"You condemn it [polygamy]?"*
> **Hinckley:** *"I condemn it. Yes, as a practice, because I think it is not doctrinal."*

Contrary to President Hinckley's statement, we still have Doctrine & Covenants 132 in our canonized scriptures. We're also still practicing plural marriage in the Temples by permitting men to be sealed to more than one woman (so long as only one is living). Apostles Elder Oaks, Elder Perry, and Elder Nelson are modern examples of LDS polygamists in that they're sealed to multiple women.

Polygamy is doctrinal. Polygamy is not doctrinal. Yesterday's doctrine is today's false doctrine. Yesterday's prophets are today's heretics.

4. BLACKS BAN

As you know, for close to 130 years blacks were not only banned from holding the priesthood but black individuals and black families were blocked from the saving ordinances of the Temple. Every single prophet from Brigham Young all the way to Harold B. Lee kept this ban in place.

Prophets, Seers, and Revelators of 2013 – in the Church's December 2013 *Race and the Priesthood*[17] essay – disavowed the "theories" of yesterday's Prophets, Seers, and Revelators for their theological, institutional, and doctrinal racist teachings and "revelation."

Yesterday's racist doctrine and revelation is now today's "disavowed theories."

Additionally, the above-mentioned essay also withdraws "that black skin is a sign of divine disfavor or curse" while ironically contradicting the Book of Mormon itself:

2 NEPHI 5:21

> "And he had caused the cursing to come upon them, yea, even a sore cursing, because of their iniquity. For behold, they had hardened their hearts against him, that they had become like unto a flint; wherefore, as they were white, and exceedingly fair and delightsome, that they might not be enticing unto my people the Lord God did cause a skin of blackness to come upon them."

Joseph Smith permitted the priesthood to at least two black men. Elijah Abel[18] was one of them. Walker Lewis[19] was another.

So, Joseph Smith gives the priesthood to blacks. Brigham Young bans blacks. Each and every single one of the 10 prophets from Brigham Young to Harold B. Lee supported what Spencer W. Kimball referred to as a "possible error" (*Teachings of Spencer W. Kimball*, p.448-449[20]).

Heavenly Father likes blacks enough to give them the priesthood under Joseph Smith but He decides they're not okay when Brigham Young shows up. And He still doesn't think they're okay for the next 130 years and the next 9 prophets until President Kimball decides to get a revelation.

The same God who "denieth none that come unto him, black and white, bond and free, male and female[21]" is the same God who denied blacks from the saving ordinances of the Temple for 130 years. Yet, He apparently changed His mind again in 1978 about black people.

Of course, the revelation He gives to the Brethren in the Salt Lake Temple on June 1, 1978 has absolutely nothing to do with the IRS potentially revoking BYU's tax-exempt status[22], Stanford and other universities boycotting BYU athletics[23], we can't figure out

Prophets

who's black or not in Brazil [24] (São Paulo Temple dedicated/opened just a few months after revelation), and that Post-Civil Rights societal trends were against the Church's racism. I would think Christ's one true Church would have led the Civil Rights movement; not be the last major church on the planet in 1978 to adopt it.

How can we trust these "Prophets, Seers, and Revelators," who have been so wrong about so many important things for so long while claiming to be receiving revelations from God?

Yesterday's doctrine is today's false doctrine. Yesterday's 10 prophets are today's heretics.

5. MARK HOFMANN

In the early to mid-1980s, the Church paid hundreds of thousands of dollars in expensive and valuable antiquities and cash to Mark Hofmann [25] – a con man and soon-to-be serial killer – to purchase and suppress bizarre and embarrassing documents into the Church vaults that undermined and threatened the Church's story of its origins. The documents were later proven to be forgeries.

- The lack of discernment by the Brethren on such a grave threat to the Church is troubling.
- Speeches by Elder Dallin H. Oaks [26] and President Gordon B. Hinckley [27] offered apologetic explanations for troubling documents (Salamander Letter [28] and Joseph Smith III Blessing [29]) that later ended up, unbeknownst to Elder Oaks and President Hinckley at the time of their apologetic talks, being proven complete fakes and forgeries.

THE FOLLOWING IS ELDER OAKS' 1985 DEFENSE[30] OF THE FAKE SALAMANDER LETTER (WHICH OAKS EVIDENTLY THOUGHT WAS REAL AND LEGITIMATE AT THE TIME):

> "Another source of differences in the accounts of different witnesses is the different meanings that different persons attach to words. We have a vivid illustration of this in the recent media excitement about the word salamander in a letter Martin Harris is supposed to have sent to W. W. Phelps over 150 years ago. All of the scores of media stories on that subject apparently assume that the author of that letter used the word salamander in the modern sense of a 'tailed amphibian.'
>
> One wonders why so many writers neglected to reveal to their readers that there is another meaning of salamander, which may even have been the primary meaning in this context in the 1820s. That meaning, which is listed second in a current edition of Webster's New World Dictionary, is 'a spirit supposed to live in fire' (2d College ed. 1982, s.v. 'salamander'). Modern and ancient literature contain many examples of this usage.
>
> A spirit that is able to live in fire is a good approximation of the description Joseph Smith gave of the angel Moroni: a personage in the midst of a light, whose countenance was 'truly like lightning' and whose overall appearance 'was glorious beyond description' (Joseph Smith-History 1:32). As Joseph Smith wrote later, 'The first sight [of this personage] was as though the house was filled with consuming fire' (History of the Church, 4:536). Since the letter purports only to be Martin Harris's interpretation of what he had heard about Joseph's experience, the use of the words white salamander and old spirit seem understandable.
>
> In view of all this, and as a matter of intellectual evaluation, why all the excitement in the media, and why the apparent hand-wringing among those who profess friendship with or membership in the Church? The media should make more complete disclosures, but Latter-day Saint readers should also be more sophisticated in their evaluation of what they read."

So, what just happened? Elder Oaks defended and rationalized a completely fake and made up document that Mark Hofmann created while telling "Latter-day Saint readers" to be "more sophisticated in their evaluation of what they read."

- There was significant dishonesty[31] by President Hinckley on his relationship with Hofmann, his meetings, and which documents that the Church had and didn't have.

- Just hours following the bombings on the morning of October 15,

1985, murderer Mark Hofmann met with Elder Dallin H. Oaks in the Church Office Building:

> "He's just killed two people. And what does he do? He goes down to the church office building and meets with Dallin Oaks. I can't even imagine the rush, given Hofmann's frame of reference, that this would have given him. To be there standing in front of one of God's appointed apostles, after murdering two people, and this person doesn't hear any words from God, doesn't intuit a thing. For Hofmann that must have been an absolute rush. He had pulled off the ultimate spoof against God."
> – The Poet and the Murderer: A True Story of Literary Crime and the Art of Forgery, p.232

Elder Oaks had a serial murderer right in front of him in his office just hours after Hofmann killed two people (Oaks later admits this meeting [32]). What does this say about the discernment of the Brethren when they can't discern a murderer and con man, hell-bent on destroying Mormonism, right under their noses?

- Ultimately, the Church was forced to admit it had, in the First Presidency Vault, documents (McLellin Collection) that the Church previously denied it had [33]. The McLellin documents were critical for the investigation of the Hofmann murders.

- While these "Prophets, Seers, and Revelators" were being duped and conned by Mark Hofmann's forgeries over a four-year period (1981-1985), the Tanners – considered some of the biggest critics of the Church – actually came out and said that the Salamander Letter was a fake [34]. Even when the Salamander Letter proved very useful in discrediting the Church, the Tanners had better discernment than the Brethren did. While the Tanners publicly rejected the Salamander Letter, the Church continued buying fakes from Hofmann and Elder Oaks continued telling Latter-day Saints to be more sophisticated.

I'm told that prophets are just men who are only prophets when acting as such (whatever that means). I'm told that, like all prophets, Brigham Young was a man of his time. For example, I was told that Brigham Young was acting as a man when he taught that "God revealed to [him]" that "Adam is our father and God" and the "only God with whom we have to do." Never mind that Brigham taught this over the pulpit in not one but two conferences and never mind that he introduced this theology into the endowment ceremony in the Temples.

Never mind that Brigham Young made it clear that he was speaking as a prophet:

> *"I have never yet preached a sermon and sent it out to the children of men, that they may not call scripture."*
> *– Journal of Discourses* 13:95 [35]

Why would I want my kids chanting "Follow the Prophet" with such a ridiculous and inconsistent 187-year track record? What credibility do the Brethren have? Why would I want them following the prophet when a prophet is just a man of his time teaching his "theories" that will likely be disavowed by future "Prophets, Seers, and Revelators"? If his moral blueprint is not much better than that of their Sunday School teachers? If, historically speaking, the doctrine he teaches today will likely be tomorrow's false doctrine?

If Brigham Young was really a Prophet, Seer, and Revelator, would it not be unreasonable to expect that God would give him a hint that racism is not okay, sexism is not okay, blood atonement is not okay, and God's name is not "Adam"?

KINDERHOOK PLATES & TRANSLATOR CLAIMS
Concerns & Questions

"I insert fac-similes of the six brass plates found near Kinderhoook…I have translated a portion of them, and find they contain the history of the person with whom they were found. He was a descendant of Ham, through the loins of Pharaoh, King of Egypt, and that he received his Kingdom from the Ruler of heaven and earth."

— JOSEPH SMITH, JR., *HISTORY OF THE CHURCH*, VOL. 5, CHAPTER 19, P.372 [1]

"Kinderhook Plates Brought to Joseph Smith Appear to be a Nineteenth-Century Hoax."

— AUGUST 1981 *ENSIGN* [2]

1. KINDERHOOK PLATES

> *"Church historians continued to insist on the authenticity of the Kinderhook Plates until 1980 when an examination conducted by the Chicago Historical Society, possessor of one plate, proved it was a nineteenth-century creation."*
> — LDS Historian Richard Bushman, Rough Stone Rolling, p.490 [3]

FACSIMILES OF THE SIX DOUBLE-SIDED KINDERHOOK PLATES

JOSEPH SMITH'S TRANSLATION	THE HOAX UNCOVERED
"I insert facsimiles of the six brass plates found near Kinderhook... I have translated a portion of them, and find they contain the history of the person with whom they were found. He was a descendant of Ham, through the loins of Pharaoh, King of Egypt, and that he received his Kingdom from the ruler of heaven and earth." –Joseph Smith, Jr.	*The plates turned out to be a hoax. Metallurgical tests revealed the plates to be of late 19th century construction. In addition, the script was created using a 19th-century chemical etch process. In August, 1981 LDS Ensign Magazine conceded:* "Kinderhook plates bought to Joseph Smith appear to be a 19th-century hoax."

- The plates were named after the town in which they were found - Kinderhook, IL. A farmer claimed he dug the plates out of a mound. They took the plates to Joseph Smith for examination and he translated a portion.

78 *Kinderhook Plates & Translator Claims*

- Not only did Joseph not discern the fraud, he added to the fraud by "translating" the fake plates. The LDS Church now concedes it's a hoax. What does this tell us about Joseph Smith's gift of translation?

2. BOOK OF ABRAHAM

As outlined in the "Book of Abraham" section, Joseph Smith got everything wrong about the papyri, the facsimiles, the names, the gods, the scene context, the fact that the papyri and facsimiles were first century C.E. funerary text, who was male, who was female, etc. It's gibberish.

There is not one single non-LDS Egyptologist who supports Joseph's Book of Abraham, its claims, or Joseph's translations. Even LDS Egyptologists [4] acknowledge there are serious problems with the Book of Abraham and Joseph's claims.

Joseph Smith made a claim that he could translate ancient documents. This is a testable claim. Joseph failed the test with the Book of Abraham. He failed the test with the Kinderhook Plates.

With this modus operandi and track record, how can I be expected to believe that Joseph translated the keystone Book of Mormon? And that he translated with a rock in a hat?

That the gold plates that ancient prophets went through all that time and effort of making, engraving, compiling, abridging, preserving, hiding, and transporting were useless? Moroni's 5,000 mile journey lugging the gold plates from Mesoamerica (if you believe the unofficial apologists) all the way to New York to bury the plates, then come back as a resurrected angel, and instruct Joseph for 4 years only for Joseph to translate instead using just a…rock in a hat?

A rock he found digging in his neighbor's property [5] in 1822 and which he later used for treasure hunting – a year before Moroni appeared in his bedroom and 5 years before he got the gold plates and Urim and Thummim?

Joseph Smith claimed to have translated three ancient records. The Book of Abraham:

proven a fraud. The Kinderhook Plates: found to be a hoax. The Book of Mormon: the only one of the three for which we do not have the original. I'm sure he was only wrong on two out of three.

> AFTER ALL, WOULDN'T YOU BUY A THIRD CAR FROM A MAN WHO HAD ALREADY SOLD YOU TWO CLUNKERS?

TESTIMONY & SPIRITUAL WITNESS
Concerns & Questions

"We should not just go on our own feelings on everything…Granted, our feelings can be wrong; of course they can be wrong…We do indeed advocate the full use of the Holy Spirit to guide us to truth. How does the Holy Spirit work? How does He testify of truth and witness unto us? Through feelings…"

– FAIRMORMON BLOG, *CAN WE TRUST OUR FEELINGS?*[1]

"Our unique strength is the ability to touch the hearts and minds of our audiences, evoking first feeling, then thought and, finally, action. We call this uniquely powerful brand of creative 'HeartSell'® - strategic emotional advertising that stimulates response."

– LDS CHURCH OWNED BONNEVILLE COMMUNICATIONS[2]

"Feelings Aren't Facts."[3]
– BARTON GOLDSMITH, PH.D., PSYCHOTHERAPIST

1. Every major religion has members who claim the same thing: God or God's spirit bore witness to them that their religion, prophet/pope/leaders, book(s), and teachings are true.

2. Just as it would be arrogant for a FLDS member, a Jehovah's Witness, a Catholic, a Seventh-day Adventist, or a Muslim to deny a Latter-day Saint's spiritual experience and testimony of the truthfulness of Mormonism, it would likewise be arrogant for a Latter-day Saint to deny others' spiritual experiences and testimonies of the truthfulness of their own religion. Yet, every religion cannot be right and true together.

> ### LDS MEMBER IN 2017
> *I know that Joseph Smith was a true prophet. I know the Church of Jesus Christ of Latter-day Saints is the one and only true Church. I know the Book of Mormon is true. I know that Thomas S. Monson is the Lord's true Prophet today.*
>
> ### FLDS MEMBER IN 2017
> *I know that Joseph Smith was a true prophet. I know the Fundamentalist Church of Jesus Christ of Latter-Day Saints is the one and only true Church. I know the Book of Mormon is true. I know that Warren Jeffs is the Lord's true Prophet today.*
>
> ### RLDS MEMBER IN 1975
> *I know that Joseph Smith was a true prophet. I know the Reorganized Church of Jesus Christ of Latter Day Saints is the one and only true Church. I know the Book of Mormon is true. I know that W. Wallace Smith[4] is the Lord's true Prophet today.*
>
> ### LDCJC MEMBER IN 2017
> *I know that Joseph Smith was a true prophet. I know The Latter Day Church of Jesus Christ[5] is the one and only true Church. I know the Book of Mormon and the Book of Jeraneck are true. I know that Matthew P. Gill is the Lord's true Prophet, Seer, Revelator, and Translator today.*

Same method: read, ponder, and pray. Different testimonies. All four testimonies cannot simultaneously be true. Is this the best God can come up with in revealing His truth to His children? Only .2% of the world's population are members of God's one true Church. This is God's model and standard of efficiency?

Praying about the truthfulness of the Book of Mormon does not follow that the LDS Church is true. The FLDS also believe in the Book of Mormon. So do dozens of Mormon splinter groups. They all believe in the divinity of the Book of Mormon as well. Praying about the first vision: Which account is true? They can't all be correct together as they conflict with one another.

3. If God's method to revealing truth is through feelings, it is a very ineffective and unreliable method. We have thousands of religions and billions of members of those religions saying that their truth is God's only truth and everyone else is wrong because they felt God or God's spirit reveal the truth to them. Each religion has believers who believe that their spiritual experiences are more authentic and powerful than those of the adherents of other religions. They cannot all be right together, if at all.

4. Joseph Smith received a revelation, through the peep stone in his hat, to send Hiram Page and Oliver Cowdery to Toronto, Canada for the sole purpose of selling the copyright of the Book of Mormon, which is another concern in itself (why would God command to sell the copyright to His word?). The mission failed and the prophet was asked why his revelation was wrong.

Joseph decided to inquire of the Lord regarding the question. Book of Mormon witness David Whitmer testified:

> "...and behold the following revelation came through the stone: 'Some revelations are of God; and some revelations are of man: and some revelations are of the devil.' So we see that the revelation to go to Toronto and sell the copy-right was not of God, but was of the devil or of the heart of man."
> – An Address to All Believers in Christ, p.31 [6]

How are we supposed to know what revelations are from God, from the devil, or from the heart of man if even the Prophet Joseph Smith couldn't tell?

Elder Boyd K. Packer said the following:

> "Be ever on guard lest you be deceived by inspiration from an unworthy source. You can be given false spiritual messages. There are counterfeit spirits just as there are counterfeit angels. (See Moro. 7:17.) Be careful lest you be deceived, for the devil may come disguised as an angel of light.
>
> The spiritual part of us and the emotional part of us are so closely linked that is possible to mistake an emotional impulse for something spiritual. We occasionally find people who receive what they assume to be spiritual promptings from God, when those promptings are either centered in the emotions or are from the adversary."
> – The Candle of the Lord, Ensign, January 1983 [6a]

What kind of a method is this if Heavenly Father allows Satan to interfere with our direct line of communication to Him? Sincerely asking for and seeking answers?

Are we now expected to not only figure out when a prophet is speaking as a prophet and not as a man while also trying to figure out whether our answers to prayer are from God, from the devil, or from ourselves?

5. As a believing Mormon, I saw a testimony as more than just spiritual experiences and feelings. I saw that we had "evidence" and "logic" on our side based on the correlated narrative I was fed by the Church about its origins. I lost this confidence when I discovered that the gap between what the Church teaches about its origins and what the primary historical documents actually show happened, and between what history shows what happened and what science shows what happened…couldn't be further apart.

I read an experience that explains this in another way:

> *"I resigned from the LDS Church and informed my bishop that the reasons had to do with discovering the real history of the Church. When I was done, he asked about the spiritual witness I had surely received as a missionary. I agreed that I had felt a sure witness, as strong as he currently felt. I gave him the analogy of Santa; I believed in Santa until I was 12. I refused to listen to reason from my friends who had discovered the truth much earlier…I just knew. However, once I learned the facts, feelings changed. I told him that Mormons have to re-define faith in order to believe; traditionally, faith is an instrument to bridge that gap between where science, history and logic end, and what you hope to be true. Mormonism re-defines faith as embracing what you hope to be true in spite of science, fact, and history."*

6. Paul H. Dunn[7]: Dunn was a General Authority of the Church for many years. He was a very popular speaker who told powerful faith-promoting war and baseball stories. Many times Dunn shared these stories in the presence of the prophet, apostles, and seventies. Stories such as how God protected him as enemy machine-gun bullets ripped away his clothing, gear, and helmet without ever touching his skin and how he was preserved by the Lord. Members of the Church shared how they strongly felt the Spirit as they listened to Dunn's testimony and stories.

Unfortunately, Dunn was later caught lying about his war and baseball stories and was forced to apologize to the members. He became the first General Authority to gain "emeritus" status and was removed from public church life.

What about the members who felt the Spirit from Dunn's fabricated and false stories? What does this say about the Spirit and what the Spirit really is?

7. The following are counsels from members of the Quorum of the Twelve Apostles on how to gain a testimony:

> "It is not unusual to have a missionary say, 'How can I bear testimony until I get one? How can I testify that God lives, that Jesus is the Christ, and that the gospel is true? If I do not have such a testimony, would that not be dishonest?' Oh, if I could teach you this one principle: a testimony is to be found in the bearing of it!"
>
> – Boyd K. Packer, *The Quest for Spiritual Knowledge* [8]
>
> "Another way to seek a testimony seems astonishing when compared with the methods of obtaining other knowledge. We gain or strengthen a testimony by bearing it. Someone even suggested that some testimonies are better gained on the feet bearing them than on the knees praying for them."
>
> – Dallin H. Oaks, *Testimony* [9]
>
> "It may come as you bear your own testimony of the Prophet...Consider recording the testimony of Joseph Smith in your own voice, listening to it regularly...Listening to the Prophet's testimony in your own voice will help bring the witness you seek."
>
> – Neil L. Andersen, *Joseph Smith* [10]

In other words, repeat things over and over until you convince yourself that it's true. Just keep telling yourself, "I know it's true...I know it's true...I know it's true" until you actually believe it and you have a testimony that the Church is true and Joseph Smith was a prophet.

How is this honest? How is this ethical? What kind of advice are these apostles giving when they're telling you that if you don't have a testimony, bear one anyway? How is this not lying? There is a difference between saying you know something and saying you believe something.

What about members and investigators who are on the other side listening to your "testimony"? How are they supposed to know whether you actually do have a testimony of Mormonism or if you're just following Packer's, Oaks', and Andersen's counsel and you're lying your way into one?

8. There are many members who share their testimonies that the Spirit told them that they were to marry this person or go to this school or move to this location or start up this business or invest in this investment. They rely on this Spirit in making critical life decisions. When the decision turns out to be not only incorrect but disastrous, the fault lies on the individual and never on the Spirit. The individual didn't have the discernment or it was the individual's hormones talking or it was the individual's greed talking or the individual wasn't worthy at the time.

This poses a profound flaw and dilemma: if individuals can be so convinced that they're being led by the Spirit but yet be so wrong about what the Spirit tells them, how can they be sure of the reliability of this same exact process and method in telling them that Mormonism is true?

How are faith and feelings reliable pathways to truth? Is there anything one *couldn't* believe based on faith and feelings?

If faith and feelings can lead one to believe and accept the truth claims of *any* one of the hundreds of thousands of contradictory religions and thousands of contradictory gods... how then are faith and feelings reliable pathways to truth?

9. I felt the Spirit watching *Saving Private Ryan* and *Schindler's List*. Both R-rated and horribly violent movies. I also felt the Spirit watching *Forrest Gump* and the *The Lion King*. After learning these disturbing issues, I attended a conference where former Mormons shared their stories. The same Spirit I felt telling me that Mormonism is true and that Joseph Smith was a true prophet is the same Spirit I felt in all of the above experiences.

Does this mean that *The Lion King* is true? That Mufasa is real and true? Does this mean that *Forrest Gump* is real and the story happened in real life? Why did I feel the Spirit as I listened to the stories of "apostates" sharing how they discovered for themselves that Mormonism is not true? Why is this Spirit so unreliable and inconsistent? How can I trust such an inconsistent and contradictory Source for knowing that Mormonism is worth betting my life, time, money, heart, mind, and obedience to?

The following mind-blowing video [11] raises some profound and thought-provoking questions about the reliability of "a witness from the Holy Ghost" for discerning truth and reality:

CESLETTER.ORG/SPIRIT

PRIESTHOOD RESTORATION
Concerns & Questions

"The late appearance of these accounts raises the possibility of later fabrication."

— LDS HISTORIAN AND SCHOLAR RICHARD BUSHMAN *ROUGH STONE ROLLING*, P.75[1]

1. Like the first vision story, none of the members of the Church or Joseph Smith's family had ever heard prior to 1832 about a priesthood restoration from John the Baptist or Peter, James, and John. Although the priesthood is now taught to have been restored in 1829, Joseph and Oliver made no such claim until 1832, if that. Even in 1832, there were no claims of a restoration of the priesthood (just a 'reception' of the priesthood) and there certainly was no specific claims of John the Baptist, Peter, James, and John. Like the first vision accounts, the story later got more elaborate and bold with specific claims of miraculous visitations from resurrected John the Baptist, Peter, James, and John.

LDS historian and scholar, Richard Bushman, acknowledges this in Rough Stone Rolling[2]:

> "Summarizing the key events in his religious life in an 1830 statement, he mentioned translation but said nothing about the restoration of priesthood or the visit of an angel. The first compilation of revelations in 1833 also omitted an account of John the Baptist. David Whitmer later told an interviewer he had heard nothing of John the Baptist until four years after the Church's organization. Not until writing in his 1832 history did Joseph include 'reception of the holy Priesthood by the ministering of angels to administer the letter of the Gospel' among the cardinal events of his history, a glancing reference at best…The late appearance of these accounts raises the possibility of later fabrication."

Why did it take 3 plus years for Joseph or Oliver to tell members of the Church about the restoration of the priesthood under the hands of John the Baptist and Peter, James, and John?

2. David Whitmer, one of the witnesses to the Book of Mormon, had this to say about the Priesthood restoration:

> "I never heard that an Angel had ordained Joseph and Oliver to the Aaronic Priesthood until the year 1834[,] [183]5, or [183]6 – in Ohio…I do not believe that John the Baptist ever ordained Joseph and Oliver…"
> – Early Mormon Documents, 5:137[3]

3. Joseph Smith and Oliver Cowdery changed the wording of an earlier revelation when they compiled the 1835 Doctrine & Covenants, adding verses about the appearances of Elijah, John the Baptist, and Peter, James, and John as if those appearances were mentioned in the earlier revelation in the Book of Commandments, which they weren't.

Compare the 1833 Book of Commandments Chapter 28 (XXVIII)[4] to the 1835 Doctrine and Covenants Section 50 (L)⁵. The chapter in modern Doctrine and Covenants is D&C 27⁶. This section claims to be a revelation from the Lord to Joseph Smith in August 1830.

The following text is what Joseph and Oliver added to the 1830 revelation in 1835 while presenting it as if this was already part of the original revelation given to Joseph by the Lord in August 1830. Notice how it's packed with miraculous claims of visitations and receptions of authority by these resurrected beings that the original 1830 revelation does not contain.

> 2. ...and with Moroni, whom I have sent unto you to reveal the book of Mormon, containing the fulness of my everlasting gospel; to whom I have committed the keys of the record of the stick of Ephraim; and also with Elias, to whom I have committed the keys of bringing to pass the restoration of all things, or the restorer of all things spoken by the mouth of all the holy prophets since the world began, concerning the last days: and also John the son of Zacharias, which Zacharias he (Elias) visited and gave promise that he should have a son, and his name should be John, and he should be filled with the spirit of Elias; which John I have sent unto you, my servants, Joseph Smith, jr. and Oliver Cowdery, to ordain you unto this first priesthood which you have received, that you might be called and ordained even as Aaron: and also Elijah, unto whom I have committed the keys of the power of turning the hearts of the fathers to the children and the hearts of the children to the fathers, that the whole earth may not be smitten with a curse: and also, with Joseph, and Jacob, and Isaac, and Abraham your fathers; by whom the promises remain; and also with Michael, or Adam, the father of all, the prince of all, the ancient of days:
>
> 3. And also with Peter, and James, and John, whom I have sent unto you, by whom I have ordained you and confirmed you to be apostles and especial witnesses of my name, and bear the keys of your ministry: and of the same things which I revealed unto them: unto whom I have committed the keys of my kingdom, and a dispensation of the gospel for the last times; and for the fulness of times, in the which I will gather together in one all things both which are in heaven and which are on earth: and also with all those whom my Father hath given me out of the world: wherefore lift up your hearts and rejoice, and gird up your loins, and take upon you my whole armor, that ye may be able to withstand the evil day, having done all ye may be able to stand. Stand, therefore, having your loins girt about with truth; having on the breastplate of righteousness; and your feet shod with the preparation of the gospel of peace which I have sent mine angels to commit unto you, taking the

> *shield of faith wherewith ye shall be able to quench all the fiery darts of the wicked; and take the helmet of salvation, and the sword of my Spirit, which I will pour out upon you, and my word which I reveal unto you, and be agreed as touching all things whatsoever ye ask of me, and be faithful until I come, and ye shall be caught up that where I am ye shall be also. Amen.*

You can see and compare for yourself on the *Joseph Smith Papers* (LDS owned and operated) website. The direct links are above.

4. Had the restoration of the Aaronic Priesthood under the hand of John the Baptist been recorded prior to 1833, it would have been expected to appear in the Book of Commandments. However, nowhere in the Book of Commandments is this miraculous and doctrinally vital event recorded.

Had the restoration of the Melchizedek Priesthood under the hands of Peter, James, and John been recorded prior to 1833, it likewise would have been expected to appear in the Book of Commandments. However, nowhere in the Book of Commandments is this miraculous and doctrinally vital event recorded.

5. It wasn't until the 1835 edition Doctrine & Covenants that Joseph and Oliver backdated and retrofitted Priesthood restoration events to an 1829-30 time period – none of which existed in any previous Church records; including Doctrine & Covenants' precursor, Book of Commandments, nor the original Church history as published in *The Evening and Morning Star*.

6. Melchizedek Priesthood given by Lyman Wight – not Peter, James, and John:

> "During the turbulent meeting, Joseph ordained five men to the high priesthood, and Lyman Wight ordained eighteen others, including Joseph. The ordinations to the high priesthood marked a milestone in Mormon ecclesiology. Until that time, the word 'priesthood,' although it appeared in the Book of Mormon, had not been used in Mormon sermonizing or modern revelations. Later accounts applied the term retroactively, but the June 1831 conference marked its first appearance in contemporary records...
>
> The Melchizedek Priesthood, Mormons now believe, had been bestowed a year or two earlier with the visit of Peter, James, and John. If so, **why did**

contemporaries say the high priesthood was given for the first time in June 1831? Joseph Smith himself was ordained to this 'high priesthood' by Lyman Wight. If Joseph was already an elder and apostle, what was the necessity of being ordained again?"

— Rough Stone Rolling, p.157-158 [7] (emphasis added)

IF PETER, JAMES, AND JOHN ORDAINED JOSEPH SMITH TO THE MELCHIZEDEK PRIESTHOOD IN 1829, WHY DID LYMAN WIGHT ORDAIN JOSEPH SMITH TO THE MELCHIZEDEK PRIESTHOOD AGAIN IN 1831?

The actual minutes of this June 1831 conference showing "Joseph Smith jr. & Sidney Rigdon were ordained to the High Priesthood under the hand of br. Lyman Wight" can be viewed on the official *Joseph Smith Papers*[8] website.

WITNESSES
Concerns & Questions

At the end of the day? It all doesn't matter. The Book of Mormon Witnesses and their testimonies of the gold plates are irrelevant. It does not matter whether eleven 19th century treasure diggers with magical worldviews saw some gold plates or not. It doesn't matter because of this one simple fact:

JOSEPH DID NOT USE THE GOLD PLATES FOR TRANSLATING THE BOOK OF MORMON

The testimony of the Three and Eight Witnesses to the Book of Mormon is a key part to the testimonies of many members of the Church. Some even base their testimony of the truthfulness of the Book of Mormon on these 11 witnesses and their claims. As a missionary, I was instructed to teach investigators about the testimonies of the witnesses to the Book of Mormon as part of boosting the book's credibility.

There are several critical problems for relying and betting on these 19th century men as credible witnesses.

MAGICAL WORLDVIEW

In order to truly understand the Book of Mormon witnesses and the issues with their claims, one must understand the magical worldview of many people in early 19th century New England. These are people who believed in folk magic, divining rods, visions, second sight, peep stones in hats, treasure hunting (money digging or glass looking), and so on.

Many people believed in buried treasure, the ability to see spirits and their dwelling places within the local hills and elsewhere. This is one reason why treasure digging as a paid service was practiced. Joseph Smith, his father, and his brother Hyrum had engaged in treasure hunting from 1820–1827. Joseph was hired by folks like Josiah Stowell, who Joseph mentions in his history[1]. In 1826, Joseph was arrested[2] and brought to court in Bainbridge, New York on the complaint of Stowell's nephew who accused Joseph of being a "disorderly person and an imposter."

It would not have been unusual during this time for a neighbor, friend, or even a stranger to come up to you and say, "I received a vision of the Lord!" and for you to respond, in all seriousness, "Well, what did the Lord say?"

This is one of the reasons why 21st century Mormons, once including myself, are so confused and bewildered when hearing stuff like Joseph Smith using a peep stone in a hat or Oliver Cowdery using a divining rod or dowsing rod[3] such as illustrated below:

The use of divining rods (such as the one above) is actually mentioned in the scriptures. In Doctrine & Covenants 8, the following heading provides context for the discussion:

> "Revelation given through Joseph Smith the Prophet to Oliver Cowdery, at Harmony, Pennsylvania, April 1829. In the course of the translation of the Book of Mormon, Oliver, who continued to serve as scribe, writing at the Prophet's dictation, desired to be endowed with the gift of translation. The Lord responded to his supplication by granting this revelation."

The revelation states, in relevant part:

D&C 8:6-11[4]
(Emphasis Added)

6. Now this is not all thy gift; for you have another gift, which is the **gift of Aaron**; behold, it has told you many things;

7. Behold, there is no other power, save the power of God, that can cause this gift of Aaron to be with you.

8. Therefore, doubt not, **for it is the gift of God; and you shall hold it in your hands**, and **do marvelous works**; and no power shall be able to take it away out of your hands, **for it is the work of God**.

9. And, therefore, **whatsoever you shall ask me to tell you by that means, that I will grant unto you**, and you shall have knowledge concerning it.

10. Remember that **without faith you can do nothing; therefore ask in faith**. Trifle not with these things; do not ask for that which you ought not.

11. Ask that you may know the mysteries of God, and **that you may translate and receive knowledge from all those ancient records which have been hid up, that are sacred**; and according to your faith shall it be done unto you.

From the D&C 8 account, we don't really know much about what exactly the "gift of Aaron" is that Oliver Cowdery received. What is "the gift of Aaron"? The text provides several clues:

- Oliver has a history of using it, since "it has told [him] many things."
- It is "the gift of God."
- It is to be held in Oliver's hands (and kept there, impervious to any power).
- It allows Oliver to "do marvelous works."
- It is "the work of God."
- The Lord will speak through it to Oliver and tell him anything he

asks while using it.
- It works through faith.
- It enables Oliver to translate ancient sacred documents.

With only these clues, the "gift of Aaron" is difficult to identify. The task becomes much easier, however, when we look at the original revelation contained in the Book of Commandments, a predecessor volume to the Doctrine & Covenants, used by the LDS Church before 1835. Specifically, Section 7 of the Book of Commandments[5] contains wording that was changed in the Doctrine & Covenants 8[6]. The term "gift of Aaron" was originally "rod" and "rod of nature" in the Book of Commandments:

> *"Now this is not all, for you have another gift, which is the **gift of working with the rod**: behold it has told you things: behold there is no other power save God, that can cause this **rod of nature**, to work in your hands."*
> – The Book of Commandments 7:37 [7] (emphasis added)

So, what is the "gift of Aaron" mentioned in D&C 8? It is a "rod of nature."

What is a "rod of nature"? It is a divining rod or dowsing rod as illustrated in the above images, which Oliver Cowdery used to hunt for buried treasure.

Cowdery's use of a divining rod to search for buried treasure evokes similar images of Joseph Smith hunting for treasure with a peep stone in a hat. Oliver also wished to use his divining rod, in the same way Joseph Smith used his stone and hat, to translate ancient documents. Doctrine & Covenants Section 8 indicates that the Lord, through Joseph Smith, granted Oliver's request to translate using a...rod.

If Oliver Cowdery's gift was really the use of a divining rod – and it was – then this tells us that the origins of the Church are much more rooted in folk magic and superstition than we've been led to believe by the LDS Church's whitewashing of its origins and history.

WITNESSES

We are told that the witnesses never disavowed their testimonies, but we have not come to know these men or investigated what else they said about their experiences.

They are 11 witnesses to the Book of Mormon: Martin Harris, Oliver Cowdery, Hiram Page, David Whitmer, John Whitmer, Christian Whitmer, Jacob Whitmer, Peter Whitmer Jr., Hyrum Smith, Samuel Smith, and Joseph Smith Sr. – who all shared a common worldview of second sight, magic, and treasure digging – which is what drew them together in 1829.

The following are several facts and observations on three of the Book of Mormon Witnesses:

MARTIN HARRIS

Martin Harris was anything but a skeptical witness. He was known by many of his peers as an unstable, gullible, and superstitious man. Brigham Young once said of Martin:

> "As for Martin Harris, he had not much to apostatize from; he possessed a wild, speculative brain. I have heard Joseph correct him and exhort him to repentance for teaching false doctrines."
> – Brigham Young Addresses, Vol. 4, 1860-1864, Elden J. Watson, p.196-199 [8]

Reports assert that he and the other witnesses never literally saw the gold plates, but only an object said to be the plates, covered with a cloth.

Additionally, Martin Harris had a direct conflict of interest in being a witness. He was deeply financially invested in the Book of Mormon as he mortgaged his farm to finance the book.

The following are some accounts of the superstitious side of Martin Harris:

> "Once while reading scripture, he reportedly mistook a candle's sputtering as a sign that the devil desired him to stop. Another time he excitedly awoke from his sleep believing that a creature as large as a dog had been upon his chest, though a nearby associate could find nothing to confirm his fears. Several hostile and perhaps unreliable accounts told of visionary experiences with Satan and Christ, Harris once reporting that Christ had been poised on a roof beam."

— *Martin Harris: Mormonism's Early Convert*, BYU Professor Ronald W. Walker, p.34-35 [9]

"No matter where he went, he saw visions and supernatural appearances all around him. He told a gentleman in Palmyra, after one of his excursions to Pennsylvania, while the translation of the Book of Mormon was going on, that on the way he met the Lord Jesus Christ, who walked along by the side of him in the shape of a deer for two or three miles, talking with him as familiarly as one man talks with another."
— John A. Clark letter, August 31, 1840 in Early Mormon Documents 2:271

"According to two Ohio newspapers, shortly after Harris arrived in Kirtland he began claiming to have 'seen Jesus Christ and that he is the handsomest man he ever did see. He has also seen the Devil, whom he described as a very sleek haired fellow with four feet, and a head like that of a Jack-ass.'"
— Early Mormon Documents 2:271, note 32

Before Harris became a Mormon, he had already changed his religion [10] at least five times. After Joseph's death, Harris continued this earlier pattern by joining and leaving 5 more different sects, including that of James Strang (whom Harris went on a mission to England for), other Mormon offshoots, and the Shakers. Not only did Harris join other religions, he testified and witnessed for them. It has been reported that Martin Harris "declared repeatedly that he had as much evidence for a Shaker book he had as for the Book of Mormon" (The Braden and Kelly Debate, p.173).

In addition to his devotion to self-proclaimed prophet James Strang, Martin Harris was a follower to another self-proclaimed Mormon prophet by the name of Gladden Bishop [11]. Like Strang, Bishop claimed to have plates, a Urim and Thummim, and that he was receiving revelation from the Lord. Martin was one of Gladden Bishop's witnesses [12] to his claims.

If someone testified to you of an unusual spiritual encounter he had, but he also told you that he...

- Conversed with Jesus who took the form of a deer
- Saw the devil with his four feet and donkey head
- Chipped off a chunk of a stone box that would mysteriously move beneath the ground to avoid capture
- Interpreted simple things like a flickering of a candle as a sign of the devil
- Had a creature appearing on his chest that no one else could see

...would you believe his claims? Or would you call the nearest mental hospital?

With inconsistencies, a conflict of interest, magical thinking, and superstition like this, exactly what credibility does Martin Harris have and why should I believe him?

DAVID WHITMER

> "David claimed in early June 1829 before their group declaration that he, Cowdery, and Joseph Smith observed 'one of the Nephites' carrying the records in a knapsack on his way to Cumorah. Several days later this trio perceived 'that the Same Person was under the shed' at the Whitmer farm."
> – An Insider's View of Mormon Origins, p.179

> "In 1880, David Whitmer was asked for a description of the angel who showed him the plates. Whitmer responded that the angel 'had no appearance or shape.' When asked by the interviewer how he then could bear testimony that he had seen and heard an angel, Whitmer replied, 'Have you never had impressions?' To which the interviewer responded, 'Then you had impressions as the Quaker when the spirit moves, or as a good Methodist in giving a happy experience, a feeling?' 'Just so,' replied Whitmer."
> – Interview with John Murphy, June 1880, EMD 5:63

A young Mormon lawyer, James Henry Moyle, who interviewed Whitmer in 1885, asked if there was any possibility that Whitmer had been deceived. "His answer was unequivocal...

Witnesses **99**

that he saw the plates and heard the angel with unmistakable clearness." But Moyle went away "not fully satisfied...It was more spiritual than I anticipated." – Moyle diary, June 28, 1885, EMD 5:141

Whitmer's testimony also included the following:

> "*If you believe my testimony to the Book of Mormon; if you believe that God spake to us three witnesses by his own voice, then I tell you that in June, 1838, God spake to me again by his own voice from the heavens and told me to 'separate myself from among the Latter Day Saints, for as they sought to do unto me, so it should be done unto them.'*"
> – David Whitmer, An Address to All Believers in Christ [13] (promoting his Whitmerite sect)

If David Whitmer is a credible witness, why are we only using his testimony of the Book of Mormon while ignoring his other testimony claiming that God Himself spoke to Whitmer "by his own voice from the heavens" in June 1838, commanding Whitmer to apostatize from the Lord's one and only true Church?

OLIVER COWDERY

Like Joseph and most of the Book of Mormon witnesses, Oliver Cowdery and his family were treasure hunters. Oliver's preferred tool of trade, as mentioned above, was the divining rod. He was known as a "rodsman." Along with the witnesses, Oliver held a magical worldview.

Also, Oliver Cowdery was not an objective and independent witness. As scribe for the

Book of Mormon, co-founder of the Church, and cousin to Joseph Smith, a conflict of interest existed in Oliver being a witness.

SECOND SIGHT

People believed they could see things as a vision in their mind. They called it "second sight." We call it "imagination." It made no difference to these people if they saw with their natural eyes or their spiritual eyes as both were one and the same.

As mentioned previously, people believed they could see spirits and their dwelling places in the local hills along with seeing buried treasure deep in the ground. This supernatural way of seeing the world is also referred in Doctrine & Covenants as "the eyes of our understanding[14]."

If the plates and the experiences were real and tangible as 21st century Mormons are led to believe, why would the witnesses make the following kind of statements when describing the plates and the experience?

> "I never saw the golden plates, only in a visionary or entranced state."
> – EMD 2:346-347

> "While praying I passed into a state of entrancement, and in that state I saw the angel and the plates."
> – EMD 2:346-347

> "He only saw the plates with a spiritual eye"
> – Joseph Smith Begins His Work, Vol. 1, 1958

> "I saw them with the eye of faith."
> – John A. Clark to Dear Brethren, 31 Aug. 1840, Episcopal Recorder (Philadelphia) 18 (12 Sept. 1840): 98

> "As shown in the vision"
> – Zenas H. Gurley, Jr., Interview with David Whitmer on January 14, 1885

> "...when I came to hear Martin Harris state in public that he never saw the plates with his natural eyes only in vision or imagination, neither Oliver nor David & also that the eight witnesses never saw them & hesitated to sign that instrument for that reason, but were persuaded to do it, the last

pedestal gave way, in my view our foundation was sapped & the entire superstructure fell in heap of ruins, I therefore three week since in the Stone Chapel...renounced the Book of Mormon...after we were done speaking M Harris arose & said he was sorry for any man who rejected the Book of Mormon for he knew it was true, he said he had hefted the plates repeatedly in a box with only a tablecloth or a handkerchief over them, but he never saw them only as he saw a city throught [sic] a mountain. And said that he never should have told that the testimony of the eight was false, if it had not been picked out of — — — [him/me?] but should have let it passed as it was..."
— Letter from Stephen Burnett to "Br. Johnson," April 15, 1838, in Joseph Smith Letter Book, p. 2

The foreman in the Palmyra printing office that produced the first Book of Mormon said that Harris *"used to practice a good deal of his characteristic jargon about 'seeing with the spiritual eye,' and the like."*
— Mormonism: Its Origin, Rise, and Progress, p.71[15]

Two other Palmyra residents said that Harris told them that he had seen the plates with "the eye of faith" or "spiritual eyes"
— EMD 2:270 and 3:22

John H. Gilbert, the typesetter for most of the Book of Mormon, said that he had asked Harris, *"Martin, did you see those plates with your naked eyes?" According to Gilbert, Harris "looked down for an instant, raised his eyes up, and said, 'No, I saw them with a spiritual eye."*
— EMD 2:548

If these witnesses literally really saw the plates like everyone else on the planet sees tangible objects...why strange statements like, "I never saw them only as I see a city through a mountain"? What does that even mean? I have never seen a city through a mountain. Have you?

Why all these bizarre statements from the witnesses if the plates were real and the event literal?

Why would you need a vision or supernatural power to see real physical plates that Joseph said were in a box that he carried around? When Martin Harris was asked, "But did you see them [plates] with your natural, your bodily eyes, just as you see this pencil-case in my hand? Now say no or yes to this." Martin answered, "I did not see them as I do that pencil-case, yet I saw them with the eye of faith; I saw them just as distinctly as I see anything around me, though at the time they were covered over with a cloth." – Origin and History of the Mormonites, p.406 [16]

Why couldn't Martin just simply answer "yes"?

JAMES STRANG AND VOREE PLATES WITNESSES

James Strang,[17] and his claims are fascinating. He was basically Joseph Smith 2.0 – but with a twist. Like Joseph, Strang did the following:

- Claimed that he was visited by an angel who reserved plates for him to translate into the word of God. "The record which was sealed from my servant Joseph. Unto thee it is reserved."
- Received the "Urim and Thummim".
- Produced 11 witnesses who testified that they too had seen and inspected ancient metal plates.
- Introduced new scripture. After unearthing the plates (the same plates as Laban from whom Nephi took the brass plates in Jerusalem), Strang translated it into scripture called the "Book of the Law of the Lord[18]."
- Established a new Church: The Church of Jesus Christ of Latter Day Saints (Strangite)[19]. Its headquarters is still today in Voree, Wisconsin.

Like the Book of Mormon, the Book of the Law of the Lord has the testimony of its Witnesses[20] in its preface:

Witnesses **103**

TESTIMONY

Be it known unto all nations, kindreds, tongues and people, to whom this Book of the Law of the Lord shall come, that James J. Strang has the plates of the ancient Book of the Law of the Lord given to Moses, from which he translated this law, and has shown them to us. We examined them with our eyes, and handled them with our hands. The engravings are beautiful antique workmanship, bearing a striking resemblance to the ancient oriental languages; and those from which the laws in this book were translated are eighteen in number, about seven inches and three-eights wide, by nine inches long, occasionally embellished with beautiful pictures.

And we testify unto you all that the everlasting kingdom of God is established, in which this law shall be kept, till it brings in rest and everlasting righteousness to all the faithful.

SAMUEL GRAHAM,
SAMUEL P. BACON,
WARREN POST,
PHINEAS WRIGHT,
ALBERT N. HOSMER,
EBENEZER PAGE,
JEHIEL SAVAGE.

In addition to the above 7 witnesses, there were 4 witnesses who went with Strang as they unearthed the Voree Plates [21]:

TESTIMONY OF WITNESSES TO THE VOREE PLATES [22]

On the thirteenth day of September, 1845, we, Aaron Smith, Jirah B. Wheelan, James M. Van Nostrand, and Edward Whitcomb, assembled at the call of James J. Strang, who is by us and many others approved as a Prophet and Seer of God. He proceeded to inform us that it had been revealed to him in a vision that an account of an ancient people was buried in a hill south of White River bridge, near the east line of Walworth County; and leading us to an oak tree about one foot in diameter, told us that we would find it enclosed in a case of rude earthen ware under that tree at the depth of about three feet; requested us to dig it up, and charged us to so examine the ground that we should know we were not imposed upon, and that it had not been buried there since the tree grew. The tree was surrounded by a sward of deeply rooted grass, such as is usually found in the openings, and upon the most critical examination we could not discover any indication that it had ever been cut through or disturbed.

We then dug up the tree, and continued to dig to the depth of about three feet, where we found a case of slightly baked clay containing three plates of brass. On one side of one is a landscape view of the south end of Gardner's prairie and the range of hills where they were dug. On another is a man with a crown on his head and a scepter in his hand, above is an eye before an upright line, below the sun and moon surrounded with twelve stars, at the bottom are twelve large stars from three of which pillars arise, and closely interspersed with them are seventy very small stars. The other four sides are very closely covered with what appear to be alphabetic characters, but in a language of which we have no knowledge.

The case was found imbedded in indurated clay so closely fitting it that it broke in taking out, and the earth below the soil was so hard as to be dug with difficulty even with a pickax. Over the case was found a flat stone about one foot wide each way and three inches thick, which appeared to have undergone the action of fire, and fell in pieces after a few minutes exposure to the air. The digging extended in the clay about eighteen inches, there being two kinds of earth of different color and appearance above it.

We examined as we dug all the way with the utmost care, and we say, with utmost confidence, that no part of the earth through which we dug exhibited any sign or indication that it had been moved or disturbed at any time previous. The roots of the tree stuck down on every side very closely, extending below the case, and closely interwoven with roots from other trees. None of them had been broken or cut away. No clay is found in the country like that of which the case is made.

In fine, we found an alphabetic and pictorial record, carefully cased up, buried deep in the earth, covered with a flat stone, with an oak tree one foot in diameter growing over it, with every evidence that the sense can give that it has lain there as long as that tree has been growing. Strang took no part in the digging, but kept entirely away from before the first blow was struck till after the plates were taken out of the case; and the sole inducement to our digging was our faith in his statement as a Prophet of the Lord that a record would thus and there be found.

AARON SMITH,
JIRAH B. WHEELAN,
J. M. VAN NOSTRAND,
EDWARD WHITCOMB.

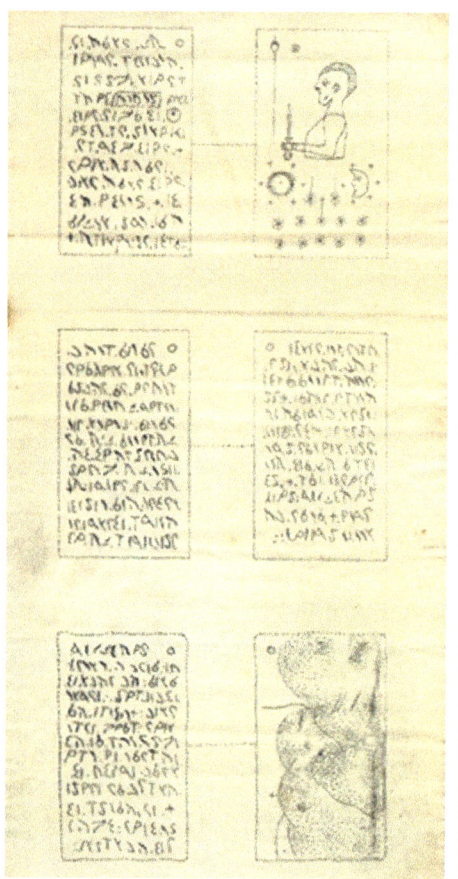
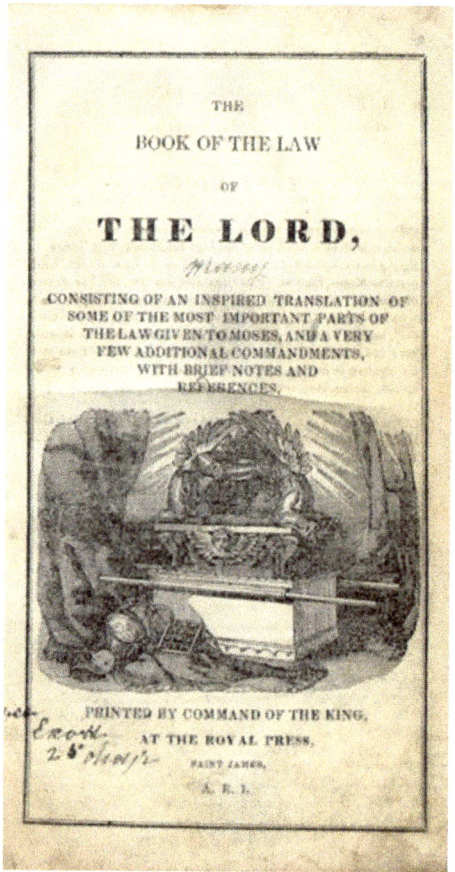

Voree Plates Facsimiles   The Book of the Law of the Lord

Like Joseph, Strang had a scribe (Samuel Graham) who wrote as Strang translated. Along with several of the witnesses, Graham was later excommunicated from Strang's Church.

There is no direct evidence that any of the above 11 Strang witnesses ever denied[23] their testimony of James Strang, the Voree Plates, Strang's church, or Strang's divine calling. Every single living Book of Mormon witness besides Oliver Cowdery accepted Strang's prophetic claim of being Joseph's true successor and joined him and his church. Additionally, every single member of Joseph Smith's family except for Hyrum's widow also endorsed, joined, and sustained James Strang as "Prophet, Seer, and Revelator."

What does this say about the credibility of the Book of Mormon witnesses if they were so easily duped by James Strang and his claims of being a prophet called of God to bring forth new scripture from ancient plates only to later turn out to be a fraud?

NO DOCUMENT OF ACTUAL SIGNATURES

The closest thing we have in existence to an original document of the testimonies of the witnesses is a printer's manuscript written by Oliver Cowdery[24] (you can see black/white photo on *Joseph Smith Papers* here[25]). Every witness name except Oliver Cowdery on that document is not signed; they are written in Oliver's own handwriting. Further, there is no testimony from any of the witnesses, with the exception of David Whitmer, directly attesting to the direct wording and claims of the manuscript or statements in the Book of Mormon.

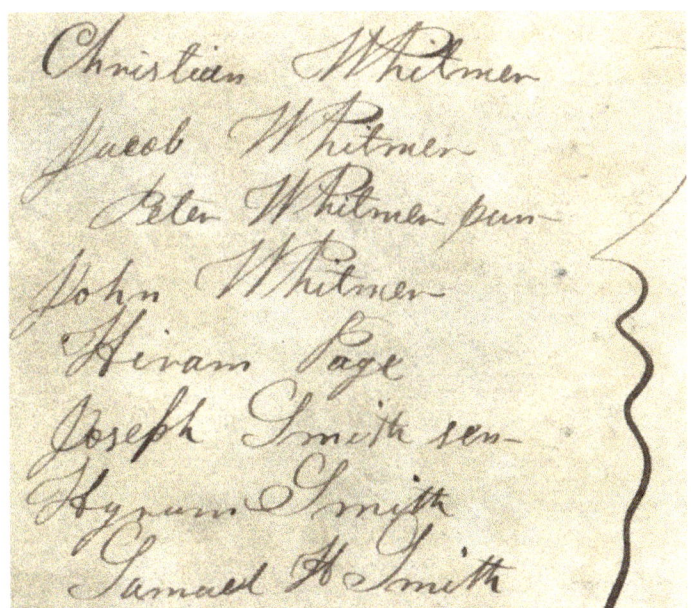

Closest Original to Testimony of Witnesses[26]

Witnesses **107**

While we have "testimonies" from the witnesses recorded in later years through interviews and second eyewitness accounts and affidavits, many of the "testimonies" given by some of the witnesses do not match the claims and wording of the preface statements in the Book of Mormon.

For example, the Testimony of Three Witnesses [27] (which includes Martin Harris) states:

> "...that we beheld and saw the plates, and the engravings thereon;"

Martin Harris:

> "...he said he had hefted the plates repeatedly in a box with only a tablecloth or a handkerchief over them, but he never saw them..."
> – Letter from Stephen Burnett to "Br. Johnson," April 15, 1838, in Joseph Smith Letter Book, p.2

> "I did not see them as I do that pencil-case, yet I saw them with the eye of faith; I saw them just as distinctly as I see anything around me, though at the time they were covered over with a cloth."
> – Origin and History of the Mormonites, p.406 [28]

There is a difference between saying you "beheld and saw the plates and the engravings thereon" and saying you "hefted the plates repeatedly in a box with only a tablecloth or a handkerchief over them" or that the plates "were covered over with a cloth" and that you "did not see them as [you] do that pencil-case, yet [you] saw them with the eye of faith" or "with a spiritual eye."

When I was a missionary, my understanding and impression from looking at the testimony of the Three [29] and Eight [30] Witnesses in the Book of Mormon was that the signatures and statements were legally binding documents in which the names represented signatures on the original document similar to those you would see on the original US Declaration of Independence [31]. This is how I presented the testimonies to investigators. According to the above manuscript that Oliver took to the printer for the Book of Mormon, they were not signatures. Since there is no document or evidence of any document whatsoever with the actual signatures of all of the witnesses, the only real testimonies we have from the witnesses are later interviews given by them and eyewitness accounts/affidavits made by others, some of which are shown previously.

From a legal perspective, the statements of the testimonies of the Three and Eight witnesses hold no credibility or weight in a court of law as there are a) no signatures of any of the witnesses except Oliver, b) no specific dates, c) no specific locations, and d) some of the witnesses made statements after the fact that contradict and cast doubt on the specific claims made in the statements contained in the preface of the Book of Mormon.

CONCLUSION

"THE WITNESSES NEVER RECANTED OR DENIED THEIR TESTIMONIES"

Neither did James Strang's witnesses; even after they were excommunicated from the church and estranged from Strang. Neither did dozens of Joseph Smith's neighbors and peers who swore and signed affidavits on Joseph's and his family's characters. Neither did many of the Shaker witnesses who signed affidavits that they saw an angel on the roof top holding the *Sacred Roll and Book* written by founder Ann Lee. Same goes for the numerous people over the centuries who claimed their entire lives to have seen the Virgin Mary and pointing to their experience as evidence that Catholicism is true.

There are also numerous witnesses who have never recanted their sincere testimonies of seeing UFOs, Big Foot, the Loch Ness Monster, Abominable Snowman, Aliens, and so on.

It simply doesn't mean anything. People believe in false things their entire lives and never recant. Just because they never denied or recanted their testimonies does not follow that their experience and claims are authentic or that reality matches to what their perceived experience was.

PROBLEMS

1. In discussing the witnesses, we should not overlook the primary accounts of the events they testified to. The official statements published in the Book of Mormon are not dated, signed (we have no record with their signatures except for Oliver's), nor is a specific location given for where the events occurred. These are not eleven legally sworn affidavits but rather simple statements pre-written by Joseph Smith with claims of having been signed by three men and another by eight.

2. All of the Book of Mormon witnesses, except Martin Harris, were related by blood or marriage either to the Smiths or Whitmers. Oliver Cowdery (married to Elizabeth Ann Whitmer and cousin to Joseph Smith), Hiram Page (married to Catherine Whitmer), and the five Whitmers were all related by marriage. Of course, Hyrum Smith, Samuel Smith, and Joseph Smith Sr. were Joseph's brothers and father.

Mark Twain made light of this obvious problem:

> "...I could not feel more satisfied and at rest if the entire Whitmer family had testified."
> – Roughing It, p.113 [32]

3. Within eight years, all of the Three Witnesses were excommunicated from the Church. This is what Joseph Smith said about them in 1838:

> "Such characters as...John Whitmer, David Whitmer, Oliver Cowdery, and Martin Harris, are too mean to mention; and we had liked to have forgotten them."
> – History of the Church Vol. 3, Ch. 15, p.232 [33]

This is what first counselor of the First Presidency and once close associate Sidney Rigdon had to say about Oliver Cowdery and David Whitmer:

> "Oliver Cowdery, David Whitmer...united with a gang of counterfeiters, thieves, liars, and blacklegs in the deepest dye, to deceive, cheat, and defraud the saints out of their property, by every art and stratagem which wickedness could invent..."
> – February 15, 1841 Letter and Testimony, p.6-9 [34]

What does it say about the Witnesses and their characters if even the Prophet and his counselor in the First Presidency thought they were questionable and unsavory?

4. As mentioned in the above "Polygamy | Polyandry" section, Joseph was able to influence and convince many of the 31 witnesses to lie and perjure in a sworn affidavit that Joseph was not a polygamist. Is it outside the realm of possibility that Joseph was also able to influence or manipulate the experiences of his own magical thinking, treasure digging family and friends as witnesses? Biased Mormon men who already believed in second sight and who already believed that Joseph Smith was a true prophet of God?

5. If the Prophet Joseph Smith could get duped with the Kinderhook Plates, thinking that the 19th century fake plates were a legitimate record of a "descendent of Ham," how is having gullible men like Martin Harris handling the covered plates going to prove anything?

6. James Strang's claims and Voree Plates Witnesses are distinctive and more impressive compared to the Book of Mormon Witnesses:

- All of Strang's witnesses were not related to one another through blood or marriage like the Book of Mormon Witnesses were.
- Some of the witnesses were not members of Strang's church.
- The Voree Plates were displayed in a museum for both members and non-members to view and examine.
- Strang provided 4 witnesses who testified that on his instructions, they actually dug the plates up for Strang while he waited for them to do so. They confirmed that the ground looked previously undisturbed.

7. The Shakers and Ann Lee:

The Shakers felt that "Christ has made his second appearance on earth, in a chosen female known by the name of Ann Lee, and acknowledged by us as our Blessed Mother in the work of redemption" (*Sacred Roll and Book*, p.358). The Shakers had a sacred book entitled <u>A Holy, Sacred and Divine Roll and Book; From the Lord God of Heaven, to the Inhabitants of Earth</u>[35].

More than 60 individuals gave testimony to the *Sacred Roll and Book*, which was published in 1843. Although not all of them mention angels appearing, some of them tell of many angels visiting them. One woman told of eight different visions.

Here is the testimony statement (page 304 of *Sacred Roll and Book*):

> *We, the undersigned, hereby testify, that we saw the holy Angel standing upon the house-top, as mentioned in the foregoing declaration, holding the Roll and Book.*
>
> BETSEY BOOTHE.
> LOUISA CHAMBERLAIN.
> CATY DE WITT.
> LAURA ANN JACOBS.
> SARAH MARIA LEWIS.
> SARAH ANN SPENCER.
> LUCINDA MCDONIELS.
> MARIA HEDRICK.

Joseph Smith only had three witnesses who claimed to see an angel. The Shakers, however, had a large number of witnesses who claimed they saw angels and the *Sacred Roll and Book*. There are over a hundred pages of testimony from "Living Witnesses." The evidence seems to show that Martin Harris accepted the *Sacred Roll and Book* as a divine revelation. Clark Braden stated: "Harris declared repeatedly that he had as much evidence for a Shaker book he had as for the Book of Mormon" (The Braden and Kelly Debate, p.173).

Why should we believe the Book of Mormon Witnesses but not the Shakers witnesses? What are we to make of the reported Martin Harris comment that he had as much evidence for the Shaker book he had as for the Book of Mormon?

In light of the James Strang/Voree Plates witnesses, the fact that all of the Book of Mormon Witnesses – except Martin Harris – were related to either Joseph Smith or David Whitmer, along with the fact that all of the witnesses were treasure hunters who believed in second sight, and in light of their superstitions and reputations...why would anyone gamble their lives by believing in a book based on anything these men said or claimed, or what's written as the testimonies of the Witnesses in the preface of the Book of Mormon?

The mistake that is made by 21st century Mormons is that they're seeing the Book of Mormon

Witnesses as empirical, rational, nineteenth-century men instead of the nineteenth-century magical thinking, superstitious, inconsistent, and treasure digging men they were. They have ignored the peculiarities of their worldview, and by so doing, they misunderstand their experiences as witnesses.

At the end of the day? It all doesn't matter. The Book of Mormon Witnesses and their testimonies of the gold plates are irrelevant. It does not matter whether eleven 19th century treasure diggers with magical worldviews saw some gold plates or not. It doesn't matter because of this one simple fact:

JOSEPH DID NOT USE THE GOLD PLATES FOR TRANSLATING THE BOOK OF MORMON

Ancient prophets go through all the time, trouble, and effort in making, engraving, compiling, abridging, preserving, transporting, hiding, and burying gold plates.

Moroni dies and comes back as a resurrected angel to deliver the gold plates to Joseph for translating the Book of Mormon.

Joseph uses his rock and hat instead for dictating the Book of Mormon we have today.

TEMPLES & FREEMASONRY
Concerns & Questions

"*Because of their Masonic characters the ceremonies of the temple are sacred and not for the public.*"

– OCTOBER 15, 1911, MESSAGE FROM THE FIRST PRESIDENCY, 4:250[1]

1. Just seven weeks after Joseph's March 1842 Masonic initiation[2], Joseph introduced the LDS endowment ceremony in May 1842[3].

2. President Heber C. Kimball, a Mason himself and a member of the First Presidency for 21 years, made the following statement:

> "We have the true Masonry. The Masonry of today is received from the apostasy which took place in the days of Solomon, and David. They have now and then a thing that is correct, but we have the real thing."
> – *Heber C. Kimball and Family: The Nauvoo Years*, Stanley B. Kimball, p.458[4]

3. If Masonry had the original Temple ceremony but became distorted over time, why doesn't the LDS ceremony more closely resemble an earlier form of Masonry, which would be more correct rather than the exact version that Joseph Smith was exposed to in his March 1842 Nauvoo, Illinois initiation?

4. Freemasonry has zero links to Solomon's Temple. Although more a Church folklore, with origins from comments made by early Mormon Masons such as Heber C. Kimball, than being Church doctrine, it's a myth that the endowment ceremony has its origins from Solomon's Temple or that Freemasonry passed down parts of the endowment over the centuries from Solomon's Temple. Solomon's Temple was all about animal sacrifice. Freemasonry has its origins to stone tradesmen in medieval Europe[5] – not in 950 BC Jerusalem.

FairMormon admits these facts:

> "Unfortunately, there is no historical evidence to support a continuous functioning line from Solomon's Temple to the present. We know what went on in Solomon's Temple; it's the ritualistic slaughter of animals."
> – The Message and the Messenger: Latter-day Saints and Freemasonry[6]

> "Masonry, while claiming a root in antiquity, can only be reliably traced to medieval stone tradesmen."
> – Similarities Between Masonic and Mormon Temple Ritual[7]

> *"It is clear that Freemasonry and its traditions played a role in the development of the endowment ritual…"*
> – Similarities Between Masonic and Mormon Temple Ritual [8]

If there's no connection to Solomon's Temple, what's so divine about a man-made medieval European secret fraternity and its rituals?

5. Why did the Church remove the blood oath penalties and the 5 Points of Fellowship at the veil from the endowment ceremony in 1990? Both of these were 100% Masonic rituals. What does this say about the Temple and the endowment ceremony if 100% pagan Masonic rituals were in it from its inception? What does it say about the Church if it removed something that Joseph Smith said he restored and which would never again be taken away from the earth?

6. Is God really going to require individuals to know secret tokens, handshakes, and signs to get into heaven? What is the purpose of them? Doesn't Heavenly Father know our names and know us personally? Indeed, aren't the very hairs on our heads numbered? [9] And couldn't those who have left the Church and still know of the secret tokens, handshakes, and signs (or those who have watched the endowment ceremony on YouTube) benefit from that knowledge?

7. Does the eternal salvation, eternal happiness, and eternal families really depend on Masonic rituals in multi-million dollar castles? Is God really going to separate good couples and their children who love one another and who want to be together in the next life because they object to uncomfortable and strange Masonic Temple rituals and a polygamous heaven?

MASTER GIVING THE GRAND MASONIC WORD ON THE FIVE POINTS OF FELLOWSHIP.

"PETER: *'The five points of fellowship* are: inside of right foot by the side of right foot, knee to knee, breast to breast, hand to back, and mouth to ear.'"

– LDS Temple Endowment - Five Points of Fellowship, Removed 1990

"WORSHIPFUL MASTER: *'The five points of fellowship* are: foot to foot, knee to knee, breast to breast, hand to back, and cheek to cheek, or mouth to ear.'"

– Masonic Five Points of Fellowship from the 3rd Degree Master Mason Ritual

SCIENCE
Concerns & Questions

"Since the Gospel embraces all truth, there can never be any genuine contradictions between true science and true religion…I am obliged, as a Latter-day Saint, to believe whatever is true, regardless of the source."

– HENRY EYRING, *FAITH OF A SCIENTIST,* P.12,31

"Latter-day revelation teaches that there was **no death on this earth before the fall of Adam**. Indeed, death entered the world as a direct result of the Fall."

– 2017 LDS BIBLE DICTIONARY TOPIC: DEATH

"4000 B.C. – Fall of Adam"

– 2017 LDS BIBLE DICTIONARY TOPIC: CHRONOLOGY OF THE OLD TESTAMENT

"More than 90 percent of all organisms that have ever lived on Earth are extinct…At least a handful of times in the last 500 million years, 50 to more than 90 percent of all species on Earth have disappeared in a geological blink of the eye."

– NATIONAL GEOGRAPHIC, *MASS EXTINCTIONS*

The problem Mormonism encounters is that so many of its claims are well within the realm of scientific study, and as such, can be proven or disproven. To cling to faith in these areas, where the overwhelming evidence is against it, is willful ignorance, not spiritual dedication.

1. 2 Nephi 2:22[1] and Alma 12:23-24[2] state there was no death of any kind (humans, all animals, birds, fish, dinosaurs, etc.) on this earth until the "Fall of Adam," which according to D&C 77:6-7[3] occurred about 7,000 years ago. It is scientifically established that there has been life and death on this planet for billions of years. How does the Church reconcile this?

How do we explain the massive fossil evidence[4] showing not only animal deaths but also the extinctions of over a dozen different Hominid species over the span of 250,000 years prior to Adam?

2. If Adam and Eve are the first humans, how do we explain the dozen or so other Hominid species[5] who lived and died 35,000 – 2.4 million years before Adam? When did those guys stop being human?

3. Genetic science and testing has advanced significantly the past few decades. I was surprised to learn from results of my own genetic test that 1.6% of my DNA is Neanderthal[6]. How does this fact fit with Mormon theology and doctrine that I am a literal descendant of a literal Adam and Eve from about 7,000 years ago? Where do the Neanderthals fit in? How do I have pre-Adamic Neanderthal DNA and Neanderthal blood circulating my veins when this species died off about 33,000 years before Adam and Eve?

4. Other events/claims that science has discredited:
- Tower of Babel[7]: (a staple story of the Jaredites in the Book of Mormon)
- Global flood[8]: 4,500 years ago
- Noah's Ark[9]: Humans and animals having their origins from Noah's family and the animals contained in the ark 4,500 years ago. It is scientifically impossible, for example, for the bear to have evolved into several species (Sun Bear, Polar Bear, Grizzly Bear, etc.) from common ancestors from Noah's time just a few thousand years ago. There are a host of other impossibilities associated with Noah's Ark story claims.

OTHER
Concerns & Questions

"The dominant narrative is not true. It can't be sustained."
− RICHARD BUSHMAN, LDS HISTORIAN, SCHOLAR, PATRIARCH
VIDEO[1] | BUSHMAN'S AFTERMATH LETTER[2]

These concerns are secondary to all of the above. These concerns do not matter if the foundational truth claims (Book of Mormon, First Vision, Prophets, Book of Abraham, Witnesses, Priesthood, Temples, etc.) are not true.

1. CHURCH'S DISHONESTY, CENSORSHIP, AND WHITEWASHING OVER ITS HISTORY

Adding to the above deceptions and dishonesty over history (rock in hat translation, polygamy|polyandry, multiple first vision accounts, etc.), the following bother me:

2013 OFFICIAL DECLARATION 2 HEADER UPDATE DISHONESTY

OFFENDING TEXT[3]
(Emphasis Added)

"*Early in its history, Church leaders stopped conferring the priesthood on black males of African descent.* **Church records offer no clear insights into the origins of this practice.**"

In sharp contrast to the above statement:

1949 FIRST PRESIDENCY STATEMENT[4]
(Emphasis Added)

August 17, 1949

The attitude of the Church with reference to Negroes remains as it has always stood. It is not a matter of the declaration of a policy ***but of direct commandment from the Lord****, on which is founded the doctrine of the Church from the days of its organization, to the effect that Negroes may become members of the Church but that they are not entitled to the priesthood at the present time.* ***The prophets of the Lord have made several statements as to the operation of the principle. President Brigham Young said: 'Why are so many of the inhabitants of the earth cursed with a skin of blackness? It comes in consequence of their fathers rejecting the power of the holy priesthood, and the law of God. They will go down to death. And when all the rest of the children have received their blessings in the holy priesthood, then that curse will be removed from the seed of Cain, and they will then come up and possess the priesthood, and receive all the blessings which we now are entitled to.'***

> President Wilford Woodruff made the following statement: 'The day will come when all that race will be redeemed and possess all the blessings which we now have.'
>
> **The position of the Church regarding the Negro may be understood when another doctrine of the Church is kept in mind, namely, that the conduct of spirits in the premortal existence has some determining effect upon the conditions and circumstances under which these spirits take on mortality and that while the details of this principle have not been made known, the mortality is a privilege that is given to those who maintain their first estate; and that the worth of the privilege is so great that spirits are willing to come to earth and take on bodies no matter what the handicap may be as to the kind of bodies they are to secure; and that among the handicaps, failure of the right to enjoy in mortality the blessings of the priesthood is a handicap which spirits are willing to assume in order that they might come to earth. Under this principle there is no injustice whatsoever involved in this deprivation as to the holding of the priesthood by the Negroes.**
>
> *The First Presidency*

Along with the above First Presidency statement, there are many other statements and explanations made by prophets and apostles clearly "justifying" the Church's racism. So, the 2013 edition Official Declaration 2 Header in the scriptures is not only misleading, it's dishonest. We do have records – including from the First Presidency itself – with very clear insights on the origins of the ban on the blacks.

UPDATE: The Church released a *Race and the Priesthood*[5] essay which contradicts their 2013 Official Declaration 2 Header[6]. In the essay, they point to Brigham Young as the originator of the ban. Further, they effectively throw 10 latter-day "Prophets, Seers, and Revelators" under the bus as they "disavow" the "theories" that these ten men taught and justified – for 130 years – as doctrine and revelation for the Church's institutional and theological racism. Finally, they denounce the idea that God punishes individuals with black skin or that God withholds blessings based on the color of one's skin while completely ignoring the contradiction[7] of the keystone Book of Mormon teaching exactly this.

ZINA DIANTHA HUNTINGTON YOUNG

(The following is a quick biographic snapshot of Zina)

- She was married for 7.5 months and was about 6 months pregnant with her first husband, Henry Jacobs [8], when she married Joseph after being told Joseph's life was in danger from an angel with a drawn sword [9].
- After Joseph's death, Zina married Brigham Young and had a child with him while still legally married to Henry Jacobs. Brigham sent Henry on missions while being married to Zina.
- Zina would eventually become the third General Relief Society President of the Church.

ZINA'S WHITEWASHED BIOGRAPHICAL PAGE ON LDS.ORG [10]

- In the "Marriage and Family" section, it does not list Joseph Smith as a husband or concurrent husband with Henry Jacobs.
- In the "Marriage and Family" section, it does not list Brigham Young as a concurrent husband with Henry Jacobs.
- There is nothing in there about the polyandry.
- It is deceptive in stating that Henry and Zina "did not remain together" while omitting that Henry separated only after Brigham Young took his wife and told Henry that Zina was now only his (Brigham) wife.

ZINA'S INDEX FILE ON LDS-OWNED FAMILYSEARCH.ORG [11]

- It clearly shows all of Zina's husbands, including her marriage to Joseph Smith.

Why is Joseph Smith not listed as one of Zina's husbands in the "Marriage and Family" section or anywhere else on her biographical page on lds.org [12]? Why is there not a single mention or hint of polyandry on her page or in that marriage section when she was married to two latter-day prophets and having children with Brigham Young while still being married to her first husband, Henry?

BRIGHAM YOUNG SUNDAY SCHOOL MANUAL

- In the Church's Sunday School manual, *Teachings of the Presidents of the Church: Brigham Young* [13], the Church changed the word "wives" to "[wife]."
- Not only is the manual deceptive in disclosing whether or not Brigham Young was a polygamist but it's deceptive in hiding Brigham Young's real teaching on marriage:

    "The only men who become Gods, even the Sons of God, are those who

enter into polygamy."
– Journal of Discourses 11:269 [14]

CENSORSHIP

In November 2013, Church Historian Elder Steven E. Snow acknowledged the Church's censorship,[15] and pointed to the advent of the internet as the contributing factor to the Church's inability to continue its pattern of hiding information and records from members and investigators:

> "*I think* **in the past there was a tendency to keep a lot of the records closed or at least not give access to information.** *But the world has changed in the last generation* — **with the access to information on the Internet, we can't continue that pattern;** *I think we need to continue to be more open.*"

2. CHURCH FINANCES

There is zero transparency to members of the Church. Why is the one and only true Church keeping its books in the dark? Why would God's one true Church choose to "keep them in darkness[16]" over such a stewardship? History has shown time and time again that secret religious wealth is breeding ground for corruption.

The Church used to be transparent with its finances but ceased disclosures in 1959.[17]

ESTIMATED $1.5 BILLION LUXURY MEGAMALL CITY CREEK CENTER [18]

- Total Church humanitarian aid from 1985-2011: $1.4 billion.[19]
- Something is fundamentally wrong with "the one true Church" spending more on an estimated $1.5 billion dollar high-end megamall than it has in 26 years of humanitarian aid.
- For an organization that claims to be Christ's only true Church, this expenditure is a moral failure on so many different levels. For a Church that asks its members to sacrifice greatly for Temple building, such as the case of Argentinians giving the Church gold from their dental work [20] for the São Paulo Brazil Temple, this mall business is absolutely shameful.
- Of all the things that Christ would tell His prophet, the prophet buys a mall and says "Let's go shopping! [21]"? Of all the sum total of human suffering and poverty

on this planet, the inspiration the Brethren feel for His Church is to get into the declining high-end shopping mall business?

PRESIDENT HINCKLEY'S DISHONEST INTERVIEW

President Hinckley made the following dishonest statement in a 2002 interview [22] to a German journalist:

> **Reporter:** *"In my country, the…we say the people's Churches, the Protestants, the Catholics, they publish all their budgets, to all the public."*
> **Hinckley:** *"Yeah. Yeah."*
> **Reporter:** *"Why is it impossible for your Church?"*
> **Hinckley:** *"Well, we simply think that the…that information belongs to those who made the contribution, and not to the world. That's the only thing. Yes."*

Where can I see the Church's books? I've paid tithing. Where can I go to see what the Church's finances are? Where can current tithing paying members go to see the books? The answer: we can't. Even if you've made the contributions as President Hinckley stated above? Unless you're an authorized General Authority or senior Church employee in the accounting department with a Non-Disclosure Agreement? You're out of luck. President Hinckley knew this and for whatever reason made the dishonest statement.

TITHING BEFORE RENT, WATER, ELECTRICITY, AND FEEDING YOUR FAMILY

I find the following quote in the December 2012 *Ensign* [23] very disturbing:

> *"If paying tithing means that you can't pay for water or electricity, pay tithing. If paying tithing means that you can't pay your rent, pay tithing. Even if paying tithing means that you don't have enough money to feed your family, pay tithing. The Lord will not abandon you."*

This despicably dangerous idea of tithing before feeding your family was further perpetuated in the April 2017 General Conference by Elder Valeri Cordón [24]:

> *"One day during those difficult times, I heard my parents discussing whether they should pay tithing or buy food for the children. On Sunday,*

> *I followed my father to see what he was going to do. After our church meetings, I saw him take an envelope and put his tithing in it. That was only part of the lesson. The question that remained for me was what we were going to eat."*

Would a loving, kind, and empathic God really place parents in the horrible position of having to choose whether to feed their children or pay what little they have to a multi-billion luxury megamall owning church that receives an estimated $8,000,000,000 in annual tithing receipts? [25]

"Well, God tested Abraham by asking him to sacrifice his son and besides, the Lord will take care of them through the Bishop's storehouse." Yes, the same god who tested Abraham is also the same capricious god who killed innocent babies and endorsed genocide, slavery, and rape [26]. The claims, counsels, and directives of these General Authorities [27], compensated with annual six figure church salaries [28], to prioritize money before the needs, health, and well-being of children [29] is hypocritical and morally reprehensible.

Besides, whatever happened to self-sufficiency [30]? Begging the Bishop for food when you had the money for food but because you followed the above counsel and gave your food money to the Church you're now dependent on the Church for food money? If you give your food and rent money to the Church, you are not self-reliant…you are Church-reliant.

DISHONESTLY ALTERING LORENZO SNOW'S WORDS AND TEACHINGS ON TITHING

The Church took the Prophet Lorenzo Snow's 1899 General Conference Address words and deliberately omitted and replaced key words on tithing with ellipsis in its *Teachings of Presidents of the Church: Lorenzo Snow* manual.

This is what Lorenzo Snow said in his 1899 General Conference Address [31]:

> "I plead with you in the name of the Lord, and I pray that every man, woman and child who has means shall pay one-tenth of their income as a tithing."

Compare this to how the Church uses and presents Snow's exact same quote today in its *Teachings of Presidents of the Church: Lorenzo Snow* [32] manual:

> "I plead with you in the name of the Lord, and I pray that every man, woman and child … shall pay one-tenth of their income as a tithing."

The Church dishonestly alters and completely changes Lorenzo Snow's words and teaching on tithing by removing "who has means" from his 1899 General Conference quote in its *Teachings of Presidents of the Church: Lorenzo Snow* manual.

In 2012, a Latter-day Saint published an eye-opening blog post that went viral among internet Mormons: Are We Paying Too Much Tithing?[33] The article demonstrates how what is currently taught and practiced is contrary to how it was taught and practiced by the Prophet Joseph Smith and subsequent prophets, including Lorenzo Snow; whose above quote was deceptively altered and manipulated for today's tithe-paying members.

2. NAMES OF THE CHURCH

1830: CHURCH OF JESUS CHRIST
1834: THE CHURCH OF THE LATTER DAY SAINTS[34]
1838: THE CHURCH OF JESUS CHRIST OF LATTER DAY SAINTS

After revealing "Church of Jesus Christ" on April 6, 1830, Joseph Smith made the decision on May 3, 1834 to change the name of the Church to "The Church of the Latter Day Saints". Why did Joseph take the name of "Jesus Christ" out of the very name of His restored Church? The one and only true Church on the face of the earth in which Christ is the Head?

KIRTLAND TEMPLE

Four years later on April 26, 1838, the Church name was changed to "The Church of Jesus Christ of Latter Day Saints" and has remained ever since (except the hyphen was added later to be grammatically correct).

Is it reasonable to assume that God would periodically change the name of his Church? If Jesus Christ is the central character of God's religion on earth and all things are to be done in His name, is it reasonable to assume that God would instruct His Church leaders to entirely leave out the name of Jesus Christ from the period of May 3, 1834 – April 26, 1838? What possible reason could there be for the name changes?

Why would Christ instruct Joseph to name it one thing in 1830 and then change it in 1834 and then change it again in 1838? Why would the name of Christ be dropped from His one and only true Church for 4 whole years?

What does this say about a Church that claims to be restored and guided by modern revelation?

3. ANTI-INTELLECTUALISM

"SOME THINGS THAT ARE TRUE ARE NOT VERY USEFUL"

Elder Boyd K. Packer gave a talk to Church Educational System Instructors and faculty at a CES Symposium on August 22, 1981 entitled *The Mantle is Far, Far Greater Than the Intellect*[35].

Elder Packer said the following:

> "There is a temptation for the writer or the teacher of Church history to want to tell everything, whether it is worthy or faith promoting or not. Some things that are true are not very useful."

Elder Dallin H. Oaks made a similar comment in the context of Church history at a CES Symposium on August 16, 1985[36]:

> "The fact that something is true is not always a justification for communicating it."

Joseph using a rock in a hat instead of the gold plates to translate the Book of Mormon is not a useful truth? The fact that there are multiple conflicting first vision accounts is not a useful truth? The fact that Joseph Smith was involved in polyandry while hiding it from Emma, when D&C 132:61 condemns it as "adultery," is not a useful truth?

Elder Packer continues:

> "That historian or scholar who delights in pointing out the weaknesses and frailties of present or past leaders destroys faith. A destroyer of faith – particularly one within the Church, and more particularly one who is employed specifically to build faith – places himself in great spiritual jeopardy."

If facts and truths can destroy faith…what does it say about faith? If prophets of the Church conducted themselves in such a way that it can destroy faith, what does this say about the prophets?

What's interesting about Elder Packer's above quote is that he's focusing on history from the point of view that a historian is only interested in the "weaknesses and frailties of present and past leaders." Historians are also interested in things like how the Book of Mormon got translated or how many accounts Joseph gave about the foundational first vision or whether the Book of Abraham even matches the papyri and facsimiles.

Besides, it matters in the religious context what past and present leaders "weaknesses and frailties" are. If Joseph's public position was that adultery and polygamy are morally wrong and condemned by God, what does it say about him and his character that he did exactly that in the dark while lying to Emma and everyone else about it? How is this not a useful truth?

A relevant hypothetical example to further illustrate this point: The prophet or one of the apostles gets caught with child pornography on his hard drive. This matters, especially in light of his current position, status, and teachings on morality. Just because a leader wears a religious hat does not follow that they're exempt from history and accountability from others.

Further, testimonies are acquired in part by the recitation of a historical narrative. Missionaries recite the narrative about Joseph Smith searching and praying for answers, about acquiring the gold plates and translating the Book of Mormon, about the Priesthood being restored along with other foundational narratives.

Why should investigators and members not learn the correct and candid version of that historical narrative, for better or for worse? Are members and investigators not entitled to a truthful accounting of the real origins of Mormonism?

The question should not be whether it's faith promoting or not to share ugly but truthful facts. The question should be: Is it the honest thing to do?

CRITICIZING LEADERS

Elder Dallin H. Oaks made the following disturbing comment in the PBS documentary, *The Mormons*[37]:

> "It is wrong to criticize the leaders of the Church, even if the criticism is true."

RESEARCHING "UNAPPROVED" MATERIALS ON THE INTERNET

Elder Quentin L. Cook made the following comment in the October 2012 General Conference[38]:

> "Some have immersed themselves in internet materials that magnify, exaggerate, and in some cases invent shortcomings of early Church leaders. Then they draw incorrect conclusions that can affect testimony. Any who have made these choices can repent and be spiritually renewed."

President Dieter F. Uchtdorf said the following in his CES talk "What is Truth?[39]" (33:00):

> "…Remember that in this age of information there are many who create doubt about anything and everything at any time and every place. You will find even those who still claim that they have evidence that the earth is flat. That the moon is a hologram. It looks like it a little bit. And that certain movie stars are really aliens from another planet. And it is always good to keep in mind just because something is printed on paper, appears on the internet, is frequently repeated or has a powerful group of followers doesn't make it true."

Why does it matter whether information was received from a stranger, television, book, magazine, comic book, napkin, and yes, the internet? They are all mediums or conduits of information. It's the information itself, its accuracy, and its relevance that matters.

Elder Neil L. Andersen made the following statement in the October 2014 General Conference[40] specifically targeting the medium of the internet in a bizarre attempt to discredit the internet as a reliable source for getting factual and truthful information:

> "We might remind the sincere inquirer that Internet information does not have a 'truth' filter. Some information, no matter how convincing, is simply not true."

UPDATE: Ironically, the only way for members to directly read the Church's admissions and validations of yesterday's "anti-Mormon lies" is by going on the internet to the Gospel Topics Essays [41] section of the Church's website. The essays and their presence on lds.org have disturbed and shocked many members – some to the point of even believing that the Church's website has been hacked.

With all this talk from General Authorities against the internet and daring to be balanced by looking at what both defenders and critics are saying about the Church, it is as if questioning and researching and doubting is now the new pornography.

Truth has no fear of the light. President George A. Smith said:

> "If a faith will not bear to be investigated; if its preachers and professors are afraid to have it examined, their foundation must be very weak."
> – Journal of Discourses 14:216 [42]

A church that is afraid to let its people determine for themselves truth and falsehood in an open market is a church that is insecure and afraid of its own truth claims.

Under Elder Cook's counsel, FairMormon and unofficial LDS apologetic websites are anti-Mormon sources that should be avoided. Not only do they introduce to Mormons "internet materials that magnify, exaggerate, and in some cases invent shortcoming of early Church leaders" but they provide asinine "faithful answers" with logical fallacies and omissions while leaving members confused and hanging with a bizarre version of Mormonism.

What about the disturbing information about early Church leaders and the Church which are not magnified, or exaggerated, or invented? What about the disturbing facts that didn't come from the flat-earthers or moon-hologramers but instead from the Church itself? Are those facts invalid when someone discovers them on the internet?

What happens when a member comes across the Church's *Book of Mormon Translation* [43] essay where they learn – for the first time in their lives – that the Book of Mormon was not translated with gold plates as depicted in Sunday Schools, *Ensigns*, MTC, General Conference addresses, or Visitor Centers?

Or the Church's *Race and the Priesthood* [44] essay where yesterday's prophets, seers, and revelators are thrown under the bus over their now disavowed "theories"?

Or the *Translation and Historicity of the Book of Abraham* [45] essay and that the Book of Abraham and its facsimiles do not match what Joseph Smith translated?

Or the *Plural Marriage in Kirtland and Nauvoo* [46] essay where they learn the real origins of polygamy and the disturbing details of how Joseph practiced it? That Joseph was married to other living men's wives and young girls as young as 14-years-old behind Emma's back? That God sent an angel with a drawn sword threatening Joseph?

Or any of the other troubling essays[47], for that matter?

Is this member in need of repentance for discovering and being troubled by all the inconsistencies and deceptions? Why is the member required to repent for discovering verifiable facts and for coming to the same logical conclusion about the LDS Church's dominant narrative that Mormon historian, scholar, and patriarch Richard Bushman did?

> *"The dominant narrative is not true. It can't be sustained."* [48]

Most of the main information and facts that I discovered and confirmed online about the Church is now found from Church sources, Church-friendly sources, and neutral sources.

"And it is always good to keep in mind just because something is printed on paper, appears on the Internet, is frequently repeated or has a powerful group of followers doesn't make it true." Exactly - the exact same can be said of Mormonism and lds.org.

GOING AFTER MEMBERS WHO PUBLISH OR SHARE THEIR QUESTIONS, CONCERNS, AND DOUBTS

THE SEPTEMBER SIX[49]

"The September Six were six members of The Church of Jesus Christ of Latter-day Saints who were excommunicated or disfellowshipped by the Church in September 1993, allegedly for publishing scholarly work on Mormonism or critiquing Church doctrine or leadership."

A few months before the September Six, Elder Boyd K. Packer made the following comment regarding the three "enemies" of the Church:

> *"The dangers I speak of come from the gay-lesbian movement, the feminist movement (both of which are relatively new), and the ever present challenge from the so-called scholars or intellectuals."*
>
> – Boyd K. Packer, All-Church Coordinating Council, May 18, 1993 [50]

STRENGTHENING THE CHURCH MEMBERS COMMITTEE (SCMC) [51]

The spying and monitoring arm of the Church. It is secretive and most members have been unaware of its existence since its creation in 1985 after Ezra Taft Benson became president. Elder Jeffrey R. Holland admitted it still exists[52] in March 2012. The historical evidence and the September Six points to SCMC's primary mission being to hunt and expose intellectuals and/or disaffected members who are influencing other members to think and question, despite Elder Holland's claim that it's a committee primarily to fight against polygamy.

"WHEN THE PROPHET SPEAKS THE DEBATE IS OVER"

N. Eldon Tanner, first counselor in the First Presidency, gave a First Presidency Message in the August 1979 *Ensign*[53] that includes the following statement:

> *"When the prophet speaks the debate is over."*

Some things that are true are not very useful + Censorship + Deceptively altering past quotes + Prioritizing tithing before food and shelter + It is wrong to criticize leaders of the Church, even if the criticism is true + Spying and monitoring on members + Intellectuals are dangerous + "us versus them" rhetoric + When the prophet speaks the debate is over + Obedience is the First Law of Heaven[54] = Policies and practices you'd expect to find in a totalitarian system such as North Korea or George Orwell's *1984*[55]; not from the gospel of Jesus Christ.

As a believing member, I was deeply offended by the accusation that the Church was a cult. "How can it be a cult when we're good people who are following Christ, focusing on family, and doing good works in and out of a church that bears His name? When we're 15 million members[56]? What a ridiculous accusation."

It was only after seeing all of the problems with the Church's foundational truth claims and discovering, for the first time, the SCMC[57] and the anti-intellectualism going on behind the scenes that I could clearly see the above cultish aspects of the Church and why people came to the conclusion that Mormonism is a cult.

CONCLUSION

"Mormonism, as it is called, must stand or fall on the story of Joseph Smith. He was either a Prophet of God, divinely called, properly appointed and commissioned or he was one of the biggest frauds this world has ever seen. There is no middle ground. If Joseph was a deceiver, who willfully attempted to mislead people, then he should be exposed, his claims should be refuted, and his doctrines shown to be false…"

– PRESIDENT JOSEPH FIELDING SMITH, *DOCTRINES OF SALVATION*, P.188 [1]

When I first discovered that gold plates were not used to translate the Book of Mormon, that Joseph Smith started polygamy and disturbingly practiced it in ways I never could have imagined, and that Joseph's Book of Abraham translations and claims are gibberish...I went into a panic. I desperately needed answers and I needed them immediately. Among the first sources I looked to for answers were official Church sources such as Mormon.org and LDS.org. I couldn't find them.

I then went to FairMormon and Neal A. Maxwell Institute (formerly FARMS).

FairMormon and these unofficial apologists have done more to destroy my testimony than any "anti-Mormon" source ever could. I find their version of Mormonism to be alien and foreign to the Chapel Mormonism that I grew up in attending Church, seminary, reading scriptures, General Conferences, EFY, Church history tour, mission, and BYU. It frustrates me that apologists use so many words in their attempts to redefine words and their meanings. Their pet theories, claims, and philosophies of men mingled with scripture are not only contradictory to the scriptures and Church teachings I learned through correlated Mormonism...they're truly bizarre.

I am amazed to learn that, according to these unofficial apologists, translate doesn't really mean translate, horses aren't really horses (they're tapirs[2]), chariots aren't really chariots (since tapirs can't pull chariots[3] without wheels[4]), steel isn't really steel, the Hill Cumorah isn't really in New York (it's possibly in Mesoamerica), Lamanites aren't really the principal ancestors of the Native American Indians, marriage isn't really marriage (if they're Joseph's plural marriages? They're mostly non-sexual spiritual sealings), and yesterday's prophets weren't really prophets when they taught today's false doctrine.

Why is it that I had to first discover all of this – from the internet – at 31-years-old after over 20 years of high activity in the Church? I wasn't just a seat warmer at Church. I've read the scriptures several times. I've read hundreds of "approved" Church books. I was an extremely dedicated missionary who voluntarily asked to stay longer in the mission field. I was very interested in and dedicated to the Gospel.

How am I supposed to feel about learning about these disturbing facts at 31-years-old? After making critical life decisions based on trust and faith that the Church was telling me the complete truth about its origins and history? After many books, seminary, EFY, Church history tour, mission, BYU, General Conferences, scriptures, *Ensigns,* and regular Church attendance?

So, putting aside the absolute shock and feeling of betrayal in learning about all of this information that has been kept concealed and hidden from me by the Church my entire life, I am now expected to go back to the drawing board. Somehow, I am supposed to rebuild my testimony on newly discovered information that is not only bizarre and alien to the Chapel Mormonism I had a testimony of; it's almost comical.

I'm now supposed to believe that Joseph has the credibility of translating ancient records when the Book of Abraham and the Kinderhook Plates destroy this claim? That Joseph has the character and integrity to take him at his word after seeing his deliberate deception in hiding and denying polygamy and polyandry for at least 10 years of his adult life? How he backdated and retrofitted the Aaronic and Melchizedek Priesthood restoration events as if they were in the Book of Commandments all along? And I'm supposed to believe with a straight face that Joseph using a rock in a hat is legit? Despite this being the exact same method he used to con people out of their money during his treasure hunting days? Despite this ruining the official story of ancient prophets and Moroni investing all of that time and effort into gold plates, which were not used because Joseph's face was stuffed in a hat?

I'm supposed to sweep under the rug the inconsistent and contradictory first vision accounts and just believe anyway? I'm supposed to believe that these men who have been wrong about so many important things and who have not prophesied, "seered," or revealed much in the last 170 or so years are to be sustained as "prophets, seers, and revelators"?

I'm supposed to believe the scriptures have credibility after endorsing so much rampant immorality, violence, and despicable behavior[5]? When it says that the earth is only 7,000 years old[6] and that there was no death before then? Or that Heavenly Father is sitting on a throne with an erect penis when all evidence points to it being the pagan Egyptian god of sex, Min? The "most correct book on earth" Book of Mormon going through over 100,000 changes[7] over the years? After going through so many revisions and still being incorrect? Noah's ark and the global flood are literal events? Tower of Babel is a literal event? The Book of Mormon containing 1769 King James Version edition translation errors and 1611 King James Version translators' italics while claiming to be an ancient record?

That there's actually a polygamous god who revealed a Warren Jeffs style revelation on polygamy that Joseph pointed to as a license to secretly marry other living men's wives and young girls and teenagers? That this god actually threatened Joseph's life with one of his angels with a sword if a newly married pregnant woman didn't agree to Joseph's marriage proposal? I'm supposed to believe in a god who was against polygamy before He was for polygamy but decided in 1890 that He was again against it?

I'm told to put these foundational problems on the shelf and wait until I die to get answers? To stop looking at the Church intellectually even though the "glory of God is intelligence[8]"? Ignore and have faith anyway?

I'm sorry, but faith is believing and hoping when there is little evidence for or against something. Delusion is believing when there is an abundance of evidence against something. To me, it is absolute insanity to bet my life, my precious time, my money, my heart, and my mind on an organization that has so many serious problematic challenges to its foundational truth claims.

There are just way too many problems. We're not just talking about one issue here. We're talking about dozens of serious issues that undermine the very foundation of the LDS Church and its truth claims.

The past year was the worst year of my life. I experienced a betrayal, loss, and sadness unlike anything I've ever known. "Do what is right; let the consequence follow.⁹" now holds a completely different meaning for me. I desperately searched for answers to all of the problems. To me, the answer eventually came but it was not what I expected…or hoped for.

As a child, it seemed so simple;
Every step was clearly marked.
Priesthood, mission, sweetheart, temple;
Bright with hope I soon embarked.
But now I have become a man,
And doubt the promise of the plan.

For the path is growing steeper,
And a slip could mean my death.
Plunging upward, ever deeper,
I can barely catch my breath.
Oh, where within this untamed wild
Is the star that led me as a child?

As I crest the shadowed mountain,
I embrace the endless sky;
The expanse of heaven's fountain
Now unfolds before my eye.
A thousand stars shine on the land,
The chart drafted by my own hand.

— THE JOURNEY[10] —

SOURCES | NOTES

To ensure updated and live links to sources, you can access all of the sources and notes online at:

CESLETTER.ORG/SOURCES

EPILOGUE

YOU PROBABLY HAVE A LOT OF QUESTIONS. HERE IS WHERE YOU CAN QUICKLY FIND ANSWERS:

CHURCH ESSAYS:
To view a list of each one of the official Church essays on lds.org verifying many of the main facts in the *CES Letter*, please visit:

CESLETTER.ORG/ESSAYS

FREQUENTLY ASKED QUESTIONS:
For answers to the most common questions, please visit:

CESLETTER.ORG/FAQ

RESOURCES:
For links to other resources – both pro-LDS and critical – please visit:

CESLETTER.ORG/RESOURCES

COMMON ATTACKS AGAINST *CES LETTER* AND JEREMY RUNNELLS:
For common attacks and lies about *CES Letter* and Jeremy Runnells, please visit:

CESLETTER.ORG/COMMON-ATTACKS

JEREMY'S DEBUNKING OF MORMON APOLOGETIC ATTACKS:
To read Jeremy's responses to unofficial Mormon apologetic attacks and claims, please visit:

CESLETTER.ORG/DEBUNKING

JEREMY'S *MORMON STORIES* INTERVIEW:
To learn more about Jeremy and his story, please visit:

CESLETTER.ORG/INTERVIEW

The most common question that Jeremy gets asked from *CES Letter* readers is: "Now What?"

"WHAT DO I DO WITH THIS INFORMATION?"

"HOW DO I TELL MY SPOUSE? MY CHILDREN? MY FAMILY?"

"WHAT WOULD YOU DO IF YOU WERE IN MY SHOES?"

"I'M SCARED...I DON'T KNOW WHAT TO THINK OR DO."

Jeremy T. Runnells

In response to the growing need for a quality manual to help guide individuals and families through this critically important and dangerous – but liberating – time, Jeremy has written *Now What?: Navigating Life After the Shelf Breaks*.

Having the advantage of both personal experience as well as the experiences of thousands of others who likewise have gone through the same process, Jeremy is in the unique position to not only help but to guide and coach individuals into answering this very important question for themselves.

Now What? will give you the information and tools you need to help you avoid the common pitfalls and mistakes made by so many after they've awakened to the LDS Church's truth crisis. The goal is not just healing but growth beyond.

For more information, please visit:

NOWWHATBOOK.COM

CES Letter Foundation is a 501(c)(3) nonprofit organization dedicated to liberating and empowering doubting, unorthodox, and disaffected Mormon individuals, marriages, and families through knowledge and resources.

It takes a tremendous amount of time and effort to provide and maintain effective life-changing information and resources.

Your support will allow us to continue to help the honest-in-heart seekers of truth find the knowledge and resources they need to pick up the pieces and to lay a solid foundation of healing and growth for themselves and their families.

If *CES Letter, Debunking FairMormon*, etc. have added value to your life, please consider paying it forward by making a tax deductible charitable donation to the *CES Letter Foundation* today.

CESLETTER.ORG/DONATE

ABOUT THE AUTHOR

Born and raised in Southern California, Jeremy Runnells was a seventh generation Mormon of Pioneer heritage who reached every Mormon youth milestone. An Eagle Scout, Returned Missionary, BYU alumnus, Jeremy was married in the San Diego Temple with expectations and plans of living Mormonism for the rest of his life. In February 2012, Jeremy experienced an awakening to the LDS Church's truth crisis, which subsequently led to a faith transition that summer. In the spring of 2013, Jeremy was approached and asked by a CES Director to share his concerns and questions about the LDS Church's origins, history, and current practices. In response, Jeremy wrote what later became virally known as the *CES Letter* (originally titled *Letter to a CES Director*). The CES Director responded that he read the "very well-written" letter and that he would provide Jeremy with a response. Unfortunately, no response ever came.

In the spring of 2016, after years of silence and refusal to answer his sincere questions, the LDS Church attempted to excommunicate Jeremy for "apostasy." Disgusted with the LDS Church's attempt to smear his name while still refusing to answer questions, Jeremy reclaimed his own power and authority during the kangaroo court by excommunicating the LDS Church from his life (resignation). This is all recorded and documented and can be found at www.cesletter.org/resign

To learn more about Jeremy's story and journey: www.cesletter.org/interview

> "I believe that members and investigators deserve to have all of the information on the table, to be able to make a fully-informed and balanced decision as to whether or not they want to commit their hearts, minds, time, talents, income, and lives to Mormonism."

CES Letter is licensed under a Creative Commons Attribution-NonCommercial-ShareAlike 4.0 International License.

You may share, distribute, alter, and build upon this work so long as you respect the following:

- Do not put "Jeremy Runnells" or "*CES Letter*" or "*Letter to a CES Director*" in your new work or imply that the above support or endorse your new work in any way. The only authorized use of the above names in your work is for attribution purposes.
- Do not use "*CES Letter*" or "*Letter to a CES Director*" or imply that your work is a prequel or sequel to the *CES Letter* (example: CES Letter – Part 2) in your new work.
- Do not use the *CES Letter* book cover (or imitation of it) or branding or brand colors.
- Do not sell, print, or offer existing *CES Letter* or your new work for profit or commercial purposes.
- Do not set up or offer *CES Letter* for mass print on print-on-demand services or publishers.
- Attribute all materials and art in *CES Letter* to its respective owners and sources.

FAIR USE:

CES Letter may contain copyrighted material the use of which has not always been specifically authorized by the copyright owner. CES Letter Foundation, a 501(c)(3) nonprofit entity, is making such material available in an effort to advance understanding of human rights, social justice, scientific, and religious issues. *CES Letter* is a Creative Commons work – available for free in the public domain – of criticism, commentary, research and nonprofit education and thus constitutes a 'Fair Use' of any such copyrighted material as provided in the United States Copyright Act of 1976, 17 U.S.C. § 107.

DISCLAIMER:

The information contained in *CES Letter* is for educational purposes only. The author and *CES Letter* Foundation are in no way liable or responsible for the information or consequences that may arise from learning said information contained in *CES Letter*. While we have done everything in our power to ensure that the information is completely accurate and up-to-date, any reliance you place on such information alone is therefore strictly at your own risk. *CES Letter* should be viewed as an introduction to the issues and thus we strongly recommend that you do your own due diligence and research to confirm the facts by using both LDS/pro-LDS and critical sources to ensure accuracy and balance. Additional pro-LDS and critical resources and links can be found at www.cesletter.org/resources.

ISBN-13: 978-0-9988699-0-2 (paperback)
First Edition Printed Paperback – October 2017

COVER DESIGN:
Craig Keeling, *craigkeeling.com*

BOOK LAYOUT:
Craig Bishop, *rcraigbishop.com*

Printed in the United States of America

CPSIA information can be obtained
at www.ICGtesting.com
Printed in the USA
JSHW050204020822
28801JS00004B/19